Contemporary Quotations in Black

Contemporary Quotations in Black

Compiled and Edited by
Anita King

Greenwood Press
Westport, Connecticut • London

Library of Congress Cataloging-in-Publication Data

Contemporary quotations in Black / compiled and edited by Anita King.
    p.   cm.
  Includes bibliographical references and index.
  ISBN 0–313–29122–5 (alk. paper)
    1. Afro-Americans—Quotations. 2. Afro-Americans—Conduct of
life—Quotations. 3. Blacks—Quotations. I. King, Anita, 1931–
E184.6.C665   1997
081'.089'96073—dc21   96–47431

British Library Cataloguing in Publication Data is available.

Library of Congress Catalog Card Number: 96–47431
ISBN: 0–313–29122–5

First published in 1997

Greenwood Press, 88 Post Road West, Westport, CT 06881
An imprint of Greenwood Publishing Group, Inc.

Printed in the United States of America

The paper used in this book complies with the
Permanent Paper Standard issued by the National
Information Standards Organization (Z39.48–1984).

10 9 8 7 6 5 4 3 2 1

Copyright Acknowledgments

The editor and publisher gratefully acknowledge permission to use quotations from the following
source: Reprinted from *I Dream a World: Portraits of Black Women Who Have Changed America.*
© 1989 Brian Lanker. Reprinted by Stewart, Tabori & Chang Publishers, New York.

Cover photos, from left to right: Rita Dove; Henry Louis Gates, Jr.; Adrian Piper; Spike Lee.

Dedicated to people of color the world over.
May the words speak for themselves.

CONTENTS

INTRODUCTION

In the more than sixteen years since the publication of my first book, *Quotations in Black*, the accomplishments of African Americans have made considerable impact in all areas of mainstream American culture, from sports and the arts to the halls of academe. *Contemporary Quotations in Black* picks up in the late 1980s and the 1990s, continuing to weave a thread that is the quest for equality—the goal of all African Americans.

Whereas *Quotations in Black* concerned itself with the voices of slavery and its descendants, *Contemporary Quotations* echoes the progress and reflects a hope that continues to beat in the hearts of blacks everywhere.

The accomplishments of such African Americans as basketball's Michael Jordan, entertainer Debbie Allen, and filmmaker Spike Lee have provided role models for young black Americans. Success in their chosen fields reminds us that hard work and perseverance are mandatory, and pay off in the long run. The exemplary achievement of Nelson Mandela, now president of South Africa, leaves no doubt that one individual can make a difference.

The quotations for *Contemporary Quotations* have been selected to reflect clarity of thought, with emphasis on faith and the uplifting of African Americans in particular and humanity in general. They also reveal that racism remains alive throughout the world and that we still have some way to go before this scourge is eradicated.

Ninety percent of the quotations in this book, which are primarily from

1990 onward, come from books, interviews, magazines, newspaper articles, and speeches. They were selected on the basis of how they reflect current African-American thoughts and opinions, while at the same time evincing an honesty that has always echoed the pain of life as a black American. *Quotations in Black* dealt in a large part with the past; *Contemporary Quotations* breaks this mold and sees African Americans as world citizens.

It is only a matter of time until racism will be no more, and we can all enjoy to the fullest an expression of the wonderful, enriching diversity of the many cultures throughout the world.

HOW TO USE
CONTEMPORARY
QUOTATIONS IN BLACK

The authors are arranged alphabetically, and the place of birth is given when known. Some people represented in this book may be unfamiliar to some readers, so a short biographical note precedes each author's quotations. For ease of access through indexing, all quotations are numbered sequentially through the book. Each author's quotations are arranged chronologically, the sources they come from are identified, and dates are given whenever possible.

Example 1

178 Education empowers you: it places you in a position to verbally challenge people who are giving you a whole lot of nonsense.

American Visions (December–January 1995)

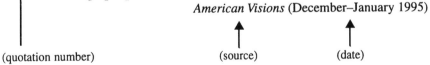

(quotation number)   (source)   (date)

Two indexes follow the numbered entries. The first is an alphabetical index of authors; numbers listed there refer to page numbers.

The second is a subject index, in which the quotations are organized under alphabetized subject and key word headings (entry words) rather than initial words. The subject headings are for the convenience of readers seeking quotable material on particular subjects rather than specific quotations. The key words provide an aid in finding specific quotes. Quotations are entered by their first lines, which are sometimes abbreviated to conform to space limitations.

Example 2

We do not allow children to fail (Collins), 159

Subject and key entries appear in alphabetical progression.

Following each index item is the author's last name and the entry numbers of the quotations.

The entry word is not spelled out in the entry itself; instead it is indicated by its initial letter, capitalized.

Example 3

ACTORS, black A are tired (McKee), 580

HANK AARON
(Mobile, Alabama, 1934–)

By the time Hank Aaron's twenty-two-year major league baseball career ended, he had a lifetime batting average of .302. Retired as a player in 1976, he became an executive with the Atlanta Braves. He was inducted into the Baseball Hall of Fame in 1982.

1   I don't have the vision or the voice of Martin Luther King or James Baldwin, or Jesse Jackson, or even of Jackie Robinson. I'm just an old ballplayer. But I learned a lot as a ballplayer. Among other things, I learned that if you manage to make a name for yourself—and if you're black, believe me, it has to be a big name—then people will start listening to what you have to say. That was why it was so important to me to break the home run record. . . . I had to break that record. I had to do it for Jackie [Robinson] and my people and myself and for everybody who ever called me nigger.

(c. 1993)

❖ ❖ ❖

KAREEM ABDUL-JABBAR
(New York City, 1947–)

Known primarily for his spectacular professional basketball career, Kareem Abdul-Jabbar is also an author and actor. He began playing in 1969 and retired after the 1989–1990 season. He is the founder of Cranberry Records, a jazz label, and has written two autobiographies.

2   I know I missed stuff. But I don't know exactly what. For most of my life I never lived in the real world.

Special Report: Sports (August–October 1990)

Hank Aaron. *Used by permission of the National Baseball Library & Archive, Cooperstown, New York.*

3   It's a burden to represent 30 million people. I'm not into that. I don't see myself as a standard bearer. I don't cater to black racism any more than I do white. I'm interested in people for what they have here and here [he touches his head and his heart with his forefinger]. I've learned over the years that the system is tolerant as long as you take unpopular stances privately, as I have.

Special Report: Sports (August–October 1990)

4   You won't win until you learn how to lose. I don't like to do it, but I can stand it. Along with everything else, you have to acquire the ability to accept defeat. No one makes it without stumbling.

Special Report: Sports (August–October 1990)

5   I have always enjoyed my height. I view it as a gift.

Special Report: Sports (August–October 1990)

6   The world chips away at the base of a champion the moment you become one. . . . That's what makes it so hard to repeat.

Kareem (1990)

7   [On a visit to Trinidad and his grandfather's grave.] Seeing the place where it all began I realize how much my grandfather had done to look out for all of us who came after him in America. I was profoundly moved.

National Geographic Traveler (July–August 1992)

8   I make no claims to perfection. I stumbled just like everyone else. But I managed to get my degree and accomplish a few things.

Washington Post (June 15, 1993)

❖ ❖ ❖

ALVIN AILEY
(Rogers, Texas, 1931–1989)

Professional dancer and choreographer, he founded and directed the Alvin Ailey American Dance Theater and appeared in theatrical and musical productions on and off Broadway. He received honorary degrees from several institutions, including Princeton University.

9   My mother was a 16-year-old country girl at my birth. She was then and still is, a gorgeous, caring, daring, fascinating, sensible, religious theatrical woman with a great sense of humor and leadership ability.

Essence (November 1988)

10   Physically, dancing hurts. There are always varying degrees of comfort and pain.

Essence (November 1988)

11   I am a person who has never completely escaped from the scars of my childhood. Racism, which leaves a shadow on one's sense of accomplishment, can make one feel like a perpetual outsider.

Essence (November 1988)

❖ ❖ ❖

DEBBIE ALLEN
(Houston, Texas, 1950–   )

Dancer, actress, choreographer, and producer-director, the multitalented Debbie Allen first came into the mass public consciousness as the dance teacher on the television show Fame. *She went on to star on Broadway and became director of over one hundred episodes of the television sitcom* A Different World.

12   My blackness is certainly a part of my makeup and it is there without being leaned on. I don't have to act black. I am black. And I think in the movies there are many parts I can play that are not written "Black."

Essence (March 1984)

13   There were times when we didn't have things. But we didn't worry about that. Because Momma made us know that we had each other and that the stars and the universe belonged to us.

Parade Magazine (November 17, 1991)

Debbie Allen. *Used by permission of the Schomburg Center for Research in Black Culture, The New York Public Library.*

14   I pounded pavements and went to every audition. That was my spirit. Work at whatever you do, whether you get paid or not.
Parade Magazine (November 17, 1991)

15   If we can't realize that we are citizens of this planet and not white people or red people or yellow people or black people, where is the possibility that we can survive together? We are one.
Parade Magazine (November 17, 1991)

16   When you look into the mirror know who is looking back at you. When you know your strengths and recognize your weaknesses, you can create art.
Parade Magazine (November 17, 1991)

❖ ❖ ❖

WALLY AMOS
(Tallahassee, Florida, 1937–   )

Wally Amos is a business entrepreneur and founder of the Famous Amos Chocolate Chip Cookie Corp., which he sold in 1985. He has established a new company, Uncle Noname, working out of Hawaii. Amos is also spokesperson for Literacy Volunteers of America.

17   There are two reasons why people fail. One is irresponsibility. The second is fear.
Parade (May 22, 1994)

18   Every experience has a lesson. . . . You give things power over yourself and then they own you.
Parade (May 22, 1994)

19   The wheels of justice grind slowly, and there's nothing you can do to hurry them.
Parade (May 22, 1994)

20   It's your mental attitude that creates results in your life.
Parade (May 22, 1994)

BENNY ANDREWS
(Madison, Georgia, 1930–   )

Benny Andrews is one of America's most respected artists. He is absorbed with the idea of a group of oppressed individuals finding release from earthly pain. That he is able to evince an excess of emotion with a minimum of abstract, gestural line is a testament to his mastery of collage as well as paint medium. He has exhibited extensively throughout the United States.

21 I do not believe we as a people can triumph if we accept the idea that just because someone has stood up to a test at one time he can disregard facing other new challenges. Paying one's dues is a lifetime proposition.

"Give Us More Space," *Between the Lines* (1978)

22 We had a sense of being made to feel important as people. We learned that people had to respect each other. We had a childhood—we enjoyed our growing up with siblings and neighbors. It gave our entire lives meaning, instilled values in us. We really did *want* things, but we appreciated what we had and learned to get the full value out of everything: garden, family, friends, job. We learned to be tolerant of those who have less.

Reckon (Fall 1995)

23 My work has always had the problem of where to place it. I will always be an outsider, and I like that.

Reckon (Fall 1995)

❖ ❖ ❖

MAYA ANGELOU
(St. Louis, Missouri, 1928–   )

Throughout her career Maya Angelou has had an important role as educator, in both the United States and abroad. In 1981 she was appointed the first Reynolds Professor of American Studies at Wake Forest

Benny Andrews. *Used by permission of Benny Andrews.*

Maya Angelou. *Used by permission of the Schomburg Center for Research in Black Culture, The New York Public Library.*

University in North Carolina. Among her best known works are And Still I Rise *(1978);* Poems *(1986);* Conversations with Maya Angelou *(1989);* I Shall Not Be Moved *(1990); and* A Brave and Startling Truth *(1995).*

24   I found out that you can fool some of the people some of the time, but you can't fool yourself.

Conversations with Maya Angelou (1989)

25   I speak to the black experience, but I am always talking about the human condition.

Conversations with Maya Angelou (1989)

26   I still feel you should rock the boat. And if you're not in it, you should turn it over.

Conversations with Maya Angelou (1989)

27   Racism is still a major issue because it is a habit.

Conversations with Maya Angelou (1989)

28   Sometimes people say they want to change, but they really want exchange. They don't want to change the system, they just want to control the existing system.

Conversations with Maya Angelou (1989)

29   We are obliged to see where we came from . . . with its failures, triumphs and exquisite little hurrahs, in order to know where we are now and to plan for tomorrow.

USA Today (May 24, 1990)

30   I am constantly startled by the healthy robustness of sexism and racism.

USA Today (May 24, 1990)

31   I never tell everything that I know. I don't even know what I know.

USA Today (May 24, 1990)

32   Most people don't really grow up. What they do is grow old, they grow tiresome even and self-righteous maybe, for it is very hard to grow. Because it means they must give up something. Usually their ignorance.

New York Newsday (January 12, 1993)

33 I am amused by our similarities just beneath the color line, the eyes, or the age, or the sex, how much we are alike. We are more alike than we are unalike.

Washington Post (January 16, 1993)

34 In my work, in everything I do, I mean to say that we human beings are more alike than we are unalike, and to use that state-ment to break down the walls we set between ourselves because we are different. I suggest that we should herald the differences, because the differences make us interesting, and also enrich and make us stronger.

Los Angeles Times (January 17, 1993)

35 I have been everything in this country. I have nursed a nation of strangers—strangers who I know—when they grew up, they would rape my daughters and kill my son. I, black woman, I.

I have fought for freedom. I have enjoyed it. I have lost it. I have been on the very bottom of the strata. I have somehow managed to keep myself intact enough to survive and to do better than that—to thrive. And to do better than that—to thrive with some passion, some compassion, some humor and some style.

Los Angeles Times (January 17, 1993)

36 We can endure, dream, fail . . . and still survive.

Washington Post (January 19, 1993)

37 Seek fashion which truly fits and befits you. You will always be in fashion only if you are true to yourself.

Wouldn't Take Nothing for My Journey Now (1993)

38 Living life as art requires a readiness to forgive.

Wouldn't Take Nothing for My Journey Now (1993)

39 Money and power can liberate only if they are used to do so. They can imprison and inhibit more finally than barred windows and iron chains.

Wouldn't Take Nothing for My Journey Now (1993)

40   The plague of racism is insidious, entering into our minds as smoothly and quietly and invisibly as floating airborne microbes enter into our bodies to find lifelong purchase in our bloodstreams.

Wouldn't Take Nothing for My Journey Now (1993)

❖ ❖ ❖

ARTHUR ASHE
(Richmond, Virginia, 1943–1993)

Arthur Ashe was the first black man to reach the top ranks of international tennis. After retirement, he established his credentials as a businessman, author, commentator, and champion of just causes.

41   I like to experience as much of life as possible. I've always felt I can sleep and rest when I'm dead; while I'm here, let's get it on and live life to the fullest.

Off the Court (1981)

42   I believe that I was destined to do more than hit tennis balls.

Off the Court (1981)

43   I have always tried to be true to myself, to pick those battles I felt were important. My ultimate responsibility is to myself. I could never be anything else.

Off the Court (1981)

44   I know that I haven't always lived without error or sin, but I also know that I have tried hard to be honest and good at all times. When I fail, my conscience comes alive.

Days of Grace: A Memoir (1993)

45   No job was beneath Daddy, as long as it was honest. He took pride in being self-sufficient.

Days of Grace: A Memoir (1993)

46 I was adamant about not giving myself over exclusively to making money. If God hadn't put me on earth mainly to stroke tennis balls, he certainly hadn't put me here to be greedy. I wanted to make a difference, however small in the world.

Days of Grace: A Memoir (1993)

47 Racism . . . is entirely made by people, and therefore it hurts and inconveniences infinitely more.

Days of Grace: A Memoir (1993)

48 Beyond the different dogmas must be a sense of yourself as created by God for a purpose, and as being under God's law at all times.

Days of Grace: A Memoir (1993)

49 Believe me, most people resist change, even when it promises to be for the better. But change will come, and if you acknowledge this simple but indisputable fact of life, and understand that you must adjust to all change, then you will have a head start.

"Letter to His Daughter, Camera," *Days of Grace: A Memoir* (1993)

50 In the 50s we were taught, being young black players, to bend over backwards as far as the rules are concerned. If a ball was close to the line, you called it good. You never argued with an official. Your decorum was above reproach. That's not natural for an athlete.

Last television interview, "Leading Questions," hosted by Michael E. Sovern, president of Columbia University (February 6, 1993)

51 I have become convinced that we blacks spend too much time on the playing field and too little time in libraries.

New York Times (February 8, 1993)

❖ ❖ ❖

GWENDOLYN CALVERT BAKER
(Ann Arbor, Michigan, 1931–   )

Gwendolyn Calvert Baker is a former schoolteacher and a past president of the New York City Board of Education. She now heads the U.S. Com-

mittee for UNICEF, the oldest and largest of thirty-five national committees that mobilize support for the United Nations Children's Fund.

52   If we can begin to pull our children away from just feeling and thinking about their plight, if we can begin to expose them to the way things are done in other places, we will begin to build a stronger group of African-American children who will be much more world-oriented.

Essence (January 1994)

❖ ❖ ❖

JAMES BALDWIN
(New York City, 1924–1987)

James Baldwin was one of the most widely quoted contemporary black writers. His considerable literary output ranged from novels and plays to magazine articles. His brilliant essay The Fire Next Time *(1962) remains a classic.*

53   [On white Americans:] They don't know how they got into the chaos of their cities, for example. But they did it—because they wanted their children to be safe, to be raised safely. So they set up their communities so that they wouldn't have to go to school with black children, whom they fear. . . . They did it inch by inch, stone by stone, decree by decree. Now their kids are deeply lost, and they can't even blame it on black people. . . . Something else is happening that will engulf them by and by.

Last interview (Paris, November 1987), *Essence* (March 1988)

54   Whites want black writers to mostly deliver something as if it were an official version of the Black experience. But no true account of Black life can be held, can be contained in the American vocabulary.

Last interview (Paris, November 1987), *Essence* (March 1988)

❖ ❖ ❖

MELBA PATTILLO BEALS
(Little Rock, Arkansas, 1941–   )

Melba Pattillo Beals was one of nine teenagers chosen to integrate Central High School in Little Rock, Arkansas, in 1957. After graduation from Central, she went on to earn a bachelor's degree from Columbia University. She has worked as a reporter for NBC and is the author of books on public relations.

55   We began moving forward [toward the high school]. The eerie silence of that moment would forever be etched in my memory. All I could hear was my own heartbeat and the sounds of boots clicking on the stone.

Warriors Don't Cry (1994)

56   Everyone seemed to be moving in slow motion as I peered past the raised bayonets of the 101st soldiers. I walked on the concrete path toward the front door of the school, the same path the Arkansas National Guard had blocked us from days before. We approached the stairs, our feet moving in unison to the rhythm of the march click-clack sound of the Screaming Eagles [soldiers of the U.S. Army 101st Airborne Division]. Step by step we climbed upward—where none of my people ever walked before as students. We stepped up to the door of Central High School and crossed the threshold into that place where angry segregationist mobs had forbidden us to go.

Warriors Don't Cry (1994)

57   The task that remains is to cope with our interdependence—to see ourselves reflected in every other human being and to respect and honor our differences.

Warriors Don't Cry (1994)

❖ ❖ ❖

HARRY BELAFONTE
(New York City, 1927–   )

Singer, producer, and political activist, Harry Belafonte has excelled as a nightclub entertainer, actor, and recording artist. In addition he has starred in films on Broadway and on television.

58   Once you get into partisan, elective politics you have to be willing to play the machine, to accept compromise. I don't have that kind of resilience.

New York Newsday (August 29, 1990)

59   Staying energized and focused is all about will; what do you want to do with your life, and do you have the will to do it? If you're willing to make the commitment and are passionate, the rest comes easy.

Family Circle (April 21, 1992)

60   I deeply believe that art has a social responsibility—not only to show how life is, but to show how life should be.

New York Daily News (November 26, 1995)

❖ ❖ ❖

DERRICK BELL
(Pittsburgh, Pennsylvania, 1930–   )

Law professor, activist, author, and leading black scholar in the United States, Derrick Bell is known for challenging the status quo and for protesting institutions through confrontation.

61   Confronting justice is risky, but with that risk comes a sense of satisfaction that may not be obtainable in any other way.

Emerge (October 1992)

62 Slavery and segregation are gone, but most whites continue to expect the society to recognize an unspoken but no less visited property right in their "whiteness." This right is recognized and upheld by courts and society like all property rights under a government created and sustained primarily for that purpose.

Race in America: The Struggle for Equality (1993)

63 Struggle does not guarantee success. We have no guarantees, only the knowledge based on the faith of our forebears who did not quit when they had every reason to do so. Their example is more than our guide. It is our mandate.

Race in America: The Struggle for Equality (1993)

64 Those of us who speak out are moved by a deep sense of the fragility of our self-worth. It is the determination to protect our sense of who we are that leads us to risk criticism, alienation, and serious loss while most others, similarly harmed, remain silent.

Race in America: The Struggle for Equality (1993)

65 The need of many whites to use race as a measure of their superiority is in itself a most serious manifestation of personal inadequacy, a deficiency worsened rather than remedied by racially discriminatory beliefs and actions.

Race in America: The Struggle for Equality (1993)

66 If the way of the peacemaker is hard, that of those who individually challenge authority is even harder.

Race in America: The Struggle for Equality (1993)

67 Through my years of challenging a host of injustices, I have learned that those in power regard every act of protest—whether against the most mundane rule or the most fundamental principle—as equally threatening.

Race in America: The Struggle for Equality (1993)

HALLE BERRY
(Cleveland, Ohio, 1968–   )

A former model and first runner-up in the Miss USA pageant, Halle Berry has appeared in a number of films, including Boomerang *and* Jungle Fever, *and played the lead role in the television miniseries* Queen.

68   It's a painful process when you have to dig deep inside yourself and find out who you are. You have to be real honest with yourself and that was a process that took me a long time.

Ebony (April 1993)

69   My mother cleared it up for me when I was very young. She said when you look in the mirror you're going to see a black woman. You're going to be discriminated against as a black woman so ultimately in this society, that's who you will be. . . . I'm neither black nor white but in the middle. But I needed to make a choice and feel part of this culture. I feel a lot of pride in being a black woman.

Ebony (April 1993)

70   I don't just want to be a face and a body. I have a voice.

Essence (June 1994)

71   I honestly wouldn't be anyone but a black woman in America right now. I feel this is *our* time to break new ground, to make statements. But first we have to . . . find the outlets for our frustrations.

Essence (June 1994)

72   My mom dealt with racism her entire life, raising two black kids alone in the '60s. She taught us that if someone's nice to you, be nice to them. If they're nasty, then don't be nice.

USA Weekend (March 8–10, 1996)

❖ ❖ ❖

MARY FRANCES BERRY
(Nashville, Tennessee, 1938–   )

Mary Frances Berry has held faculty and administrative positions at several universities and is the Geraldine R. Segal Professor of American Social Thought and professor of history at the University of Pennsylvania. Her noted works are Long Memory: The Black Experience in America *(1986), and* The Politics of Parenthood *(1993).*

73   Race is such an ancient burden that we drag around with us in this country. It's on everybody's mind almost all the time, even if they think it's not. It's part of the American psyche, to have it on your mind and to be unresolved.

I Dream a World (1989)

74   The mother-care tradition persists because we are acculturated to accept it and because it reinforces existing power arrangements. The tradition is, however, neither traditional nor necessary.

The Politics of Parenthood (1993)

75   There was a time in our country's history when fathers took responsibility for the care of their offspring. A complete reversal of roles today is neither required nor necessary. If women, however, are to have an equal opportunity for successful careers and families, both fathers and mothers must share child care.

The Politics of Parenthood (1993)

❖ ❖ ❖

UNITA BLACKWELL
(Lula, Mississippi, 1933–   )

Unita Blackwell, the first black mayor elected in Mississippi, was a key organizer of the Mississippi Freedom Democratic party. She has also been chairperson of the Black Woman Mayors' Caucus and second vice-president of the National Conference of Black Mayors.

76   I am the law. I am over the slave owners that used to be over me. I am their mayor. I'm the judge. So it has changed. It's not that subtle thing that we have overcome yet. But that physical outward thing to that mental thing that they're going to get you is not there anymore.

I Dream a World (1989)

❖ ❖ ❖

GUION S. BLUFORD
(Philadelphia, Pennsylvania, 1942–   )

As a pilot in the U.S. Air Force, Guion Bluford served in Vietnam. Later he became one of the first blacks accepted for astronaut training. His first mission was aboard Challenger *in 1983. In 1985 he was a mission specialist aboard America's first Space Lab mission.*

77   I am awed at man's ingenuity and what he can achieve. I recognized what a beautiful and fragile planet we live on. Seeing earth from 170 miles out in space is not like standing on earth and looking at the moon.

USA Today (February 1, 1983)

78   I learned to work hard for success. It was the only way I could achieve what I wanted. I also learned to be persistent and not let intermediate failures deter me from achieving a long-term goal. I learned to accept failures and successes along the way.

USA Today (February 1, 1983)

79   When you're flying in space you get a much broader perspective of the world that we live in, and I think you recognize very quickly that this planet we live on is a small planet and we have to share it together. You recognize the importance of our managing our resources as effectively as possible, as well as the importance of getting along together. We are all passengers on this planet earth.

Black Visions '90: Afro-Americans in Space Science
(February 1–28, 1990)

Guion S. Bluford. *Photo courtesy of NASA.*

80   I hope to be remembered not only as an astronaut but as an aerospace engineer, as a pilot and hopefully as a pioneer in the aerospace business.

Crisis (August–September 1995)

❖ ❖ ❖

TYRONE "Muggsy" BOGUES
(Baltimore, Maryland, 1965–   )

Tyrone "Muggsy" Bogues has been the starting point guard for the Charlotte Hornets for several seasons. At five feet three inches, Bogues is the shortest player in the history of the National Basketball Association.

81   Basketball is about talent, and heart, and desire. It's not about size. It's not a game for people who are big. It's a game for people who can play.

In the Land of Giants (1994)

82   There is nothing I like better than a challenge.

In the Land of Giants (1994)

83   Take a chance. If you fail that's alright. Success comes with failure. . . . I have certainly had my failures, my disappointments. That's when you really appreciate success. You know what it takes to get there and to sustain it.

In the Land of Giants (1994)

❖ ❖ ❖

JULIAN BOND
(Nashville, Tennessee, 1940–   )

Julian Bond was a prominent social activist during the 1960s civil rights movement. Today he writes, reviews books and films, and addresses political and social issues.

84 At our best we were and are a caring people. At our worse we were and are a narrow selfish people devoted to skin privilege and economic advantage for only a few.
"Civil Rights Then and Now," address, Philadelphia, Pennsylvania
(June 9, 1990)

85 Receiving rights others enjoy is no special benefit or badge of privilege; it is the natural order of things in a democratic society.
"Civil Rights Then and Now," address, Philadelphia, Pennsylvania
(June 9, 1990)

86 Race and racial prejudice remain the greatest determinants of life chances in America. In retrospect, we were foolish to believe a society which values material wealth over human life could be cleansed so quickly of this virus; it has proven more deadly than any other plague today.
"Civil Rights Then and Now," address, Philadelphia, Pennsylvania
(June 9, 1990)

❖ ❖ ❖

TOM BRADLEY
(Calvert, Texas, 1917–   )

In 1973 Tom Bradley was elected the first black mayor of Los Angeles, California.

87 Anybody who tries to analyze me in a simplistic way will miss the boat. I'm a very complex man in my reactions, in my emotions and in the way I do things.
Los Angeles Times (January 19, 1992)

88 It pains me to talk to a youngster who has never finished a book.
Los Angeles Times (January 19, 1992)

BARBARA BRANDON
(Long Island, New York, 1960?–)

Barbara Brandon is the first syndicated black woman cartoonist. Today her strip, "Where I'm Coming From," appears in more than fifty papers, including the Detroit Free Press *and* Baltimore Sun.

89   I'm the first [syndicated black woman cartoonist] and I'm proud of it. But this is the '90s and I have to sit back and ask "What's taking us so long?"

People Weekly (February 10, 1992)

90   When I'm dead and gone . . . folks can look at these strips and identify what black women were experiencing.

People Weekly (February 10, 1992)

❖ ❖ ❖

AVERY BROOKS
(Evansville, Indiana, 1949–)

Actor Avery Brooks has played a variety of roles, from Paul Robeson and Othello to Commander Benjamin Sisko on television's Deep Space Nine. *He has also lectured on the university circuit to students in the theater arts.*

91   I feel it's the responsibility of artists always to seek the largest forum to discuss the world in which they live.

Essence (April 1989)

92   I grew up in the context of a Black community where ideas such as dignity and integrity and proper behavior still existed. I thought that was the way the whole world was, and I will insist that, ultimately, that's the way it still is.

Essence (April 1989)

93   I do not visit schools because of charity. The fact is, I exist only in the context of my community. To survive, we must review discussions about the value of life.

Address, Courtland Milloy College (December 11, 1990)

94   Politics notwithstanding, the beacon [Paul Robeson] represented for Black people should not be forgotten. You can't think of any movement today he didn't influence: civil rights, labor, freedom for the artist—he represented them all.

Los Angeles Times (January 23, 1992)

95   You can't grow up without feeling the pervasive and unspoken racism that exists. . . . It's the way you're perceived. I cannot explain it to my children.

Los Angeles Times (January 23, 1992)

❖ ❖ ❖

DREW T. BROWN III
(New York City, 1955–   )

The son of Bundini Brown, Muhammad Ali's trainer, and Rhoda Palestine, a white Jewish woman, Drew grew up caught between two worlds. He eventually joined the U.S. Navy and became a carrier attack pilot. He went on to establish the American Dream, a program that takes him all over the country to address education issues.

96   I come from the ghetto, the projects of Harlem in New York City. Now I don't know about you, but if you think you got it bad in your area, let me tell you the rats in my school were so big, the cats carried assault weapons.

You Gotta Believe! (1991)

97   I went to your house, stepped on a roach, and your mother yelled, "Save me the white meat."

You Gotta Believe! (1991)

98   Prejudice is a human trait. It has nothing to do with color. Hitler only killed white people. He was white. Idi Amin only killed black people. He was black. Prejudice simply means you don't like yourself, so you have to put someone else down—because of how they look, feel, or act—in order to make yourself look better. Look in the mirror. If you have any of that garbage in your body, the truth is you really don't like yourself.

You Gotta Believe! (1991)

99   You can lead a horse to water, but you can't make him drink. I make him thirsty. God Bless America.

You Gotta Believe! (1991)

❖ ❖ ❖

JAMES BROWN
(Augusta, Georgia, 1934–   )

James Brown was hailed as the "Godfather of Soul" in the late 1960s and popularized the slogan, "Say it loud. I'm black and I'm proud."

100   There's something wrong with the system. It's designed for you not to make it. And if you make it, it's designed for you not to keep it. Taking James Brown out of the music business is like taking Moses out of the Bible and saying it was a complete book.

Los Angeles Times (February 9, 1989)

101   I thank God I know what I know. Everybody helps you win. But nobody helps you when you lose. So when you get back to winning again, they'll love you again.

Rolling Stone (April 6, 1989)

102   I been human all my life, but we don't get human rights.

Rolling Stone (April 6, 1989)

103   I think the record speaks clearly for itself. We can look in the mirror and tell what color we are. Remember, I'm the man who sang the song "I'm Black and I'm Proud." But I don't need to

James Brown. *Used by permission of the Schomburg Center for Research in Black Culture, The New York Public Library.*

resurrect 400 years of history to make a better tomorrow. I'm not worried about what happened yesterday. I'm looking forward to a long spiritual relationship with humanity in the future.

Los Angeles Times (February 27, 1991)

104   I'm not going to tell you what's missing in American music. I never telegraph my moves.

Los Angeles Times (February 27, 1991)

105   A man who doesn't stand for something will go for anything.

Los Angeles Times (February 27, 1991)

106   I'm no leader of no black community. I'm a role model but I don't lead. Blacks don't need no leaders, they need educators and politicians.

Details (July 1991)

❖ ❖ ❖

TONY BROWN
(Charleston, West Virginia, 1933–   )

For over twenty years Tony Brown has produced his own television show. He also writes a syndicated newspaper column and has a weekly radio program. He was the founding dean of Howard University's School of Communications, Washington, D.C.

107   If I were white, I wouldn't be unusual. I'm black and that makes me very unusual. I am not afraid of white people. I believe most black people are scared of white people. I don't think there is anything to fear. They are no better than I am. I don't think some of them are as good as I am. Black people for the most part worship whites too much. We have to learn to love ourselves.

USA Today (October 22, 1985)

108 I learned early in life that all I was going to have was what I was willing to work for.

Fortune (November 4, 1991)

109 The only thing we can depend on is ourselves.

Mother Jones (March–April 1993)

110 The black community has to shift from an obsession with racism to an obsession with education.

Mother Jones (March–April 1993)

❖ ❖ ❖

MATTHIAS BUNTY
(London, England, 1965–)

Dancer-choreographer Matthias Bunty is of Jamaican-Scottish origin. She has danced with Bill T. Jones and Twyla Tharp, in addition to having her own dance company, Harlemation. She has also appeared in two Spike Lee videos.

111 I want to bring dance to new venues—to football stadiums, shopping centers and everywhere it hasn't been. I live to see the day when dance is as accessible as a train ride. Maybe crime wouldn't be on the upswing if its protagonists were mildly associated with the internal beauty of the arts.

Interview (May 1992)

❖ ❖ ❖

YVONNE BRAITHWAITE BURKE
(Los Angeles, California, 1932–)

Yvonne Braithwaite Burke was elected to the U.S. House of Representatives in 1972. She was the first woman elected to Congress from Cal-

ifornia in twenty years. In 1978, after serving three terms, she returned to California, where she became a specialist in public finance.

112   I'm willing to take a chance because I really believe I'm going to win. But you're not going to win unless you try.

I Dream a World (1989)

113   In the South, if we had waited to change the hearts and minds of people, it would have taken two more generations. We don't have time. As far as I'm concerned you're not going to change the hearts and minds. You have to change the law.

I Dream a World (1989)

❖ ❖ ❖

CHARLES BURNETT
(Vicksburg, Mississippi, 1944–   )

Charles Burnett is a filmmaker. Among his works are My Brother's Wedding *(ca. 1985) and* To Sleep with Anger *(1990). His films are a rare testimony that the black community can, does, and will continue to exist without explicit reference to the white world that surrounds it and constrains it.*

114   I do not think that it is a bad thing to be disillusioned. You become very realistic. You learn what the odds are. It is just like picking a fight. And you need it both ways—the ideas because they give you a sense of direction and an initial purpose and a reality check. Sometimes it is good to come to terms with the reality.

Callaloo (Summer 1994)

LeVAR BURTON
(Landstuhl, Germany, 1957–   )

LeVar Burton is probably best known for his role as Lieutenant Com-
mander Geordi LaForge in the long-running television series Star Trek:
The Next Generation. *He is also host and Executive Producer of the*
Emmy Award–winning Reading Rainbow. *Burton is currently producing,*
writing, and directing his own projects.

115   I read to entertain myself, to educate myself, as a way to en-
      lighten myself—as a way to challenge my beliefs about myself.
                                          Washington Post (July 25, 1993)

116   [Television is] the most powerful tool we can possess in this
      culture, in this civilization, with which we can address social
      growth and change.
                                          Washington Post (July 25, 1993)

❖ ❖ ❖

OCTAVIA BUTLER
(Pasadena, California, 1947–   )

Octavia Butler is a science-fiction writer.

117   A science-fiction writer has the freedom to do absolutely any-
      thing. The limits are in the imagination of the writer.
                                       Black Scholar (March–April 1986)

118   I believed I was ugly and stupid, clumsy and socially hopeless.
      I also thought that everyone would notice these faults if I drew
      attention to myself. I wanted to disappear. Instead, I grew to be
      six feet tall.
                                                  Essence (May 1989)

119   Ignorance is expensive.
                                                  Essence (May 1989)

LeVar Burton. *Used by permission of LeVar Burton.*

120   I have no gift for suffering in silence. Act tough and confident, and don't talk about your doubts. If you never deal with them you may never get rid of them, but no matter. Fake everyone out. Even yourself.

Essence (May 1989)

❖ ❖ ❖

SHIRLEY CAESAR
(Durham, North Carolina, 1938–   )

Gospel singer and minister, Shirley Caesar began her gospel career in 1958, forming her own group in 1966. She has won several Grammies for her gospel recordings and is pastor of Mount Calvary Holy Church, Raleigh, North Carolina.

121   Women have a way of treating people more softly. We treat souls with kid gloves.

USA Today (October 1, 1987)

122   The majority of black churches are dancing in the spirit, and a lot of white ones are, too. . . . The dance is given to people who have the victory over their lives.

USA Today (October 1, 1987)

123   Fifty percent of my earnings I give back to the Lord to help feed the hungry, clothe the naked and even help people with housing and things of that nature.

Our Time Press (March 1996)

124   I come from a singing background, a preaching and missionary background and because I am totally committed to what I am doing it comes from the soul, from the inside.

Our Time Press (March 1996)

125   I cannot go up and try to be somebody that I am not. . . . I can't be anybody else but me.

Our Time Press (March 1996)

126   I don't have time to become bigheaded because I know that the same people who put you up will also bring you down.

Our Time Press (March 1996)

127   Everybody's on a mission of some kind.

Our Time Press (March 1996)

❖ ❖ ❖

JAMES CAMERON
(LaCrosse, Wisconsin, 1914–   )

James Cameron is the only man known to have survived a Ku Klux Klan lynching. He is the founder of America's Holocaust Museum, located in Milwaukee, Wisconsin.

128   When the question of the black man can be stripped of all its irritating and exciting causes and stereotyped images, we can then have brotherhood and peace; law can reign supreme. Then the interests of society will be promoted and the welfare of all classes of our people, because when dealing with the virtue of brotherhood, we pass beyond the limits of man-made law and deal in spiritual things that reach beyond time.

A Time of Terror (1980)

129   When they quit burning witches in Salem, they started burning blacks and Indians like they were going out of style.

A Time of Terror (1980)

130   Someday, true education will shower down upon our country and the truth will indeed make us free. We must hold on to our faith.

Letter to the editor, *Milwaukee Community Journal* (June 24, 1992)

131   Universal education must go hand-in-hand with universal safety.
Letter to the editor, *Milwaukee Community Journal* (June 24, 1992)

❖ ❖ ❖

BEBE MOORE CAMPBELL
(Philadelphia, Pennsylvania, 1950–   )

Journalist and author Bebe Moore Campbell has established herself as an important African-American writer of fiction and nonfiction. Her work has appeared in the New York Times, Washington Post, Los Angeles Times, Ms., *and* Black Enterprise.

132   Long ago I realized that love is all that is required of fatherhood, that love will spark the action that it takes to mold a child. I have grown strong and whole from the blessings of my many fathers. Everything they gave me—roughness, gruffness, awkward gentleness, the contrast to my female world, their love—is as much a part of me as my bones, my blood. I was given a rich and privileged childhood, an American childhood, a solid foundation on which to stand and, yes, even to go forward. I was guided by good men, powerful men. I was raised right.
Sweet Summer: Growing Up with and without My Dad (1989)

133   In life, the trick is just to do what's necessary to keep on living. . . . Life will give you what you deserve, even when people don't.
Your Blues Ain't Like Mine (1992)

134   Knowing who you are begins in the mind.
Your Blues Ain't Like Mine (1992)

❖ ❖ ❖

ELIZABETH CATLETT
(Washington, D.C., 1919–   )

Acclaimed for her figurative sculptures and lithographs, Elizabeth Catlett has been a prominent black artist for fifty years.

135   Individual gains are limited by group advancement.

"The Negro People and American Art at Mid-Century,"
address before the National Conference of Negro Artists (April 1961)

136   Art can't be the exclusive domain of the elect. It has to belong to everyone. Otherwise it will continue to divide the privileged from the underprivileged. Blacks from Chicanos, and both from rural, ghetto and middle-class whites. Artists should work to the end that love, peace, justice, and equal opportunity prevail all over the world; to the end that all people take joy in full participation in the rich material, intellectual, and spiritual resources of this world's lands, peoples and goods.

The Art of Elizabeth Catlett (1984)

137   Sometimes I put things away because I become frustrated to the point where I should not make decisions. This type of antagonism can be the root of creativity because it leads you to closer examinations of your approach and to alternative solutions to problems.

The Art of Elizabeth Catlett (1984)

138   I try to do art that will interest my people. I'm not trying to impress art critics or to do art for museums. People who run museums are millionaires and they have a whole other idea about art.

Washington Post (May 5, 1993)

Elizabeth Catlett. *Used by permission of Elizabeth Catlett.*

RAY CHARLES
(Albany, Georgia, 1933–   )

Raised in Greenville, Florida, Ray Charles has played piano since the age of five. At age six he contracted the glaucoma that would blind him two years later. He went on to become one of the blues legends of our time and a recipient of countless awards. His records have sold in the millions.

139   Believe me, when I was five years old I could read my ABCs. I could count before I could even go to school. Guess who I got it from? My mother.

USA Today (June 23, 1986)

140   There's such a thing as too much happiness and sadness. What I'm after is contentment.

Los Angeles Times (May 28, 1989)

141   Record executives control the money but they can't keep time.

Interview (November 1991)

142   My theory about music is if you do good music people will follow you long after you're dead.

Minneapolis Star Tribune (May 31, 1992)

❖ ❖ ❖

RuPAUL ANDRE CHARLES
(San Diego, California, 1961?–   )

RuPaul Andre Charles is best known for his success in the music, film, and entertainment industries. He is the first drag queen to become a spokesmodel for a major cosmetics company.

143   Most people are afraid of what lurks deep inside of themselves. They spend a lifetime running away from it or smothering it with

Ray Charles. *Used by permission of the Schomburg Center for Research in Black Culture, The New York Public Library.*

food, sex, drugs, or alcohol. One of life's biggest challenges is to look in the mirror, because there's really nothing to be afraid of.

Lettin' It All Hang Out (1995)

144 There is no such thing as normality—each and every one of us, if we dare to be whole, is a gorgeous peacock.

Lettin' It All Hang Out (1995)

145 There is no higher authority on the planet when it comes to deciding what's best for you, than you. Life is a banquet, so you should eat until you are full, and do as you please as long as you're not hurting anybody else.

Lettin' It All Hang Out (1995)

146 You can't get satisfaction living your life according to someone else's rules.

Lettin' It All Hang Out (1995)

❖ ❖ ❖

SEPTIMA POINSETTE CLARK
(Charleston, South Carolina, 1898–1987)

Septima Clark was an influential social activist in the 1950s and 1960s. She came to activism through teaching and remained committed to the idea that education is the key to political empowerment.

147 My husband had strong feelings against women and felt they should stay in their place, which was in the house making children or buying groceries. But the civil rights movement would never have taken off if some women hadn't spoken up.

Life (Spring 1988)

❖ ❖ ❖

XERNONA CLAYTON
(Muskogee, Oklahoma, 1930–   )

*Xernona Clayton has been an Atlanta civic leader for over two decades.
For her outstanding volunteer service as well as professional achieve-
ments, she has received innumerable awards, including* Ebony's Most
Promising Black Woman in Corporate America *(1991).*

148   I think people do *decide* to practice discrimination. It is finally a
matter of choice whether you are going to be fair-minded or big-
oted.

I've Been Marching All the Time (1991)

149   The big thing that continues to hurt is the dehumanizing *feeling*
of racism. You wonder all the time if you are going to be accepted, how you will be treated if you want to buy a house or a
car, or whether an insurance company might redline your neighborhood. . . . That kind of discrimination seems inexplicable in
1991.

I've Been Marching All the Time (1991)

150   As I look back now it pleases me to note how many changes
there have been, how many battles, large and small, have been
waged and won against racial discrimination. But I also ponder
how far we still have to go.

I've Been Marching All the Time (1991)

❖ ❖ ❖

JOHNNETTA BETSCH COLE
(Jacksonville, Florida, 1936–   )

*Johnnetta Betsch Cole was admitted to Fisk University at the age of
fifteen. She attended Oberlin College and later Northwestern University.
In 1987 she became the first African-American woman to serve as president of Spelman College, Atlanta, Georgia.*

151   In our colleges and universities, in our society, and in our world either we learn to deal with diversity or we will be unified in our destruction.

> Address, Council for Advancement and Support of Education,
> Washington, D.C. (ca. July 3, 1989)

152   It is time for us to turn inward to ourselves in search of ways to heal our own troubled communities.

> Address, NAACP Convention,
> Los Angeles, California (July 9, 1990)

❖ ❖ ❖

ROBERT COLESCOTT
(Oakland, California, 1925–   )

Few other artists in recent history have created as powerful a body of work as Robert Colescott. He received his B.A. and M.A. degrees from the University of California at Berkeley in drawing and painting. He continues to make an important contribution to contemporary American art.

153   [On two years spent in Egypt:] It was an eye-opener to spend time in a non-white society and be part of the majority. I had 3,000 years of non-European narrative art to study. I felt my identity enhanced.

> *Los Angeles Times* (January 1, 1991)

154   I am an observer in my work. I have no doctrine. I want to talk about the foolishness of it all. I want to encourage people to relate rather than to punish one another. I don't even know what to be angry at.

> *Los Angeles Times* (January 1, 1991)

MARVA COLLINS
(Monroeville, Alabama, 1936–)

Former public school teacher Marva Collins is founder of Westside Preparatory School and National Teacher Training Institute in Chicago. Her philosophy encompasses the learning of self-discipline, the value of hard work, and self-esteem.

155 Society can continue to predict, but I shall continue to determine.
USA Today (March 7, 1983)

156 I am not a quitter. There have been some hard, hard times. I have cried, but I do it privately.
USA Today (March 7, 1983)

157 We can all pay teachers to teach, but how much do you really pay a teacher to care?
"Relighting the Candles of Excellence across America,"
address at Calvin College (January 1990)

158 Life is not served to me on a proverbial platter. I will discourage being average.
"Relighting the Candles of Excellence across America,"
address at Calvin College (January 1990)

159 We do not allow children to fail.
"Relighting the Candles of Excellence across America,"
address at Calvin College (January 1990)

160 I think we all need money to survive, but we have to get with that spirit again where we want to give something back, where it's a legacy. It's our rent that we pay for our space on earth.
"Relighting the Candles of Excellence across America,"
address at Calvin College (January 1990)

161 People yield very painfully to change.
"Relighting the Candles of Excellence across America,"
address at Calvin College (January 1990)

162   Children want to and can learn. Provide them with the right environment, the right motivation, and the right material, and children will demonstrate their natural ability to excel.

Marva Collins' Way (1990)

163   It is too easy and too convenient to conclude that bad students are poorly motivated or stupid. This conclusion is a poor excuse and it runs counter to the truth. A good teacher can always make a poor student good and a good student superior.

Marva Collins' Way (1990)

❖ ❖ ❖

MARYSE CONDÉ
(Pointe à Pitre, Guadeloupe, 1936–   )

Maryse Condé is known for her books Tree of Life *(1992) and the best-seller* Segu *(1987). Since completing five plays and several novels, Condé has been teaching and lecturing at universities throughout the United States.*

164   Love comes by surprise like death. It doesn't move forward beating the *gwo-ka*. Its foot penetrates softly, softly in the loose soil of the hearts.

Crossing the Mangrove (1989)

165   We as writers . . . should try to produce a communication between people not based only on color but maybe on ethics, knowledge, sympathy. . . . If we could get rid of the trauma of color, life would be much more easy for all of us.

Callaloo (Spring 1991)

❖ ❖ ❖

BILL COSBY
(Germantown, Pennsylvania, 1937–)

Comedian, actor, writer, recording artist, and businessman, Bill Cosby is one of television's funniest and most popular entertainers. He has made more than twenty comedy albums, appeared in films, and written several books.

166   We've got to examine who and what a hero is and how far we, the fans, go in putting these people up on pedestals. They're not perfect, but then again, neither are we.

Playboy (December 1985)

167   In spite of all the love and joy and gratification that children bring, they do cause a certain amount of stress that takes its toll on parents. My wife and I have five children, and the reason we have five is that we did not want six.

Fatherhood (1986)

168   You know the only people who are *always* sure about the proper way to raise children? Those who've never had any.

Fatherhood (1986)

169   Whenever your kids are out of control, you can take comfort from the thought that even God's omnipotence did not extend to His kids. After creating heaven and earth, the oceans, and the entire animal kingdom, God created Adam and Eve. And the first thing he said was "Don't."

Fatherhood (1986)

170   Wiser men than I have thought about age and have never figured out anything to do except say, "Happy Birthday." What, after all, is old? To a child of seven ten is old; to a child of ten twenty-five is middle-aged and fifty is an archaeological exhibit.

Time Flies (1987)

171   We do need in this country more behavioral scientists; the United States of America needs to address itself to mental sickness.

Los Angeles Times (December 10, 1989)

Bill Cosby. *Used by permission of the Schomburg Center for Research in Black Culture, The New York Public Library.*

172 It's easy to blame other people, or the government for having no faith in yourself. But the expression of our mass psychosis is in our anti-social behavior.

Los Angeles Times (December 10, 1989)

173 The pen is mightier than the sword because you don't have to be there to get stabbed by the pen.

Los Angeles Times (December 10, 1989)

174 Afro-Americans are the only people who do not have any good ol' days.

Los Angeles Times (December 10, 1989)

175 The word *minority* has connotations of weakness, lesser value, self-doubt, tentativeness and powerlessness. Many of us have been a ''minority'' for so long that we have absorbed that characterization into our personalities.

Ebony (November 1990)

176 We cannot afford to settle for being just average; we must learn as much as we can to be the best that we can. The key word is *education*—that knowledge—education with maximum effort. Without it, we cannot be in charge of ourselves or anyone else.

Ebony (November 1990)

177 After you graduate today, even if you have no job, you can work at treating human beings with the values they have, made by God.

Commencement address, University of Maryland (May 19, 1992)

❖ ❖ ❖

CAMILLE COSBY
(Washington, D.C., 1945–)

An indispensable partner in the Dr. William and Dr. Camille Cosby team, Bill Cosby's wife has made a major contribution as a philanthropist and educator.

178   Education empowers you: it places you in a position to verbally challenge people who are giving you a whole lot of nonsense.

American Visions (December–January 1995)

179   I just want to be an agent for change. I want to do my part in helping people to change their negative attitudes about us as a people. And hopefully, if we have any negative attitudes about ourselves, I want to help change those, too.

American Visions (December–January 1995)

❖ ❖ ❖

ELLIS COSE
(Chicago, Illinois, 1951–   )

Ellis Cose began his career in journalism as a weekly writer for the Chicago Sun-Times; *he has been the recipient of numerous fellowships, grants, and journalism awards.*

180   America is filled with attitudes, assumptions, stereotypes, and behaviors that make it virtually impossible for blacks to believe that the nation is serious about its promise of equality—even, perhaps especially for those who have been blessed with material success.

The Rage of a Privileged Class (1993)

181   For most blacks in America, regardless of status, political persuasion, or accomplishments, the moment never arrives when race can be treated as a total irrelevancy. Instead, too often it is the only relevant factor defining our existence.

The Rage of a Privileged Class (1993)

❖ ❖ ❖

BENEDITA DA SILVA
(Rio de Janeiro, Brazil, 1942–)

Born in Chapeu Mangueira, a Rio de Janeiro slum, Benedita da Silva's first job was washing clothes. By sheer force of her personality, Benedita rose to serve once as a Rio city councilwoman and twice as national deputy. She was the first woman and black to run for mayor of Rio de Janeiro.

182 For me being black has always been a tremendous advantage. The worst thing I could do is run away from it.
Washington Post (November 15, 1992)

183 The institutional church has a hegemonic conception of a person's life. It removes people's individuality when it imposes its determinations in the name of faith which in reality are political actions that inhibit the growth of the individual as if such growth were a big sin.
Christian Century (May 5, 1993)

❖ ❖ ❖

JULIE DASH
(New York City, 1952–)

Filmmaker Dash is producer-director of Daughters of the Dust *(1992), the first nationally distributed, feature-length film by an African-American woman.*

184 With the educational system here in the United States, you grow up assuming we had no input. But we've had so much input into this society, and it's not just music and athletes. It's the language, motor habits, how we move.
Washington Post (February 28, 1992)

❖ ❖ ❖

MILES DAVIS
(Alton, Illinois, 1926–1991)

Trumpet player, composer, and bandleader, Miles Davis was a great inspiration not only to musicians the world over but to music scribes and theorists as well. His place in jazz history is ensured.

185   I said years and years ago, "Why play Beethoven when you can start something new?"
Atlanta Constitution (May 27, 1989)

186   There are only two things important to me, and that is music and black people.
Atlanta Constitution (May 27, 1989)

187   I stopped talking to the audience because they weren't coming to hear me speak but to hear the music I was playing.
Miles: The Autobiography (1989)

188   Good music is good no matter what kind of music it is.
Miles: The Autobiography (1989)

189   I never saw nothing in poverty and hard times and the blues. I never wanted that for myself. . . . When you're creating your own shit, man, even the sky ain't the limit.
Miles: The Autobiography (1989)

190   Black people are acting out roles every day in this country just to keep on getting by. If white people really knew what was on most black people's minds it would scare them to death. Blacks don't have the power to say these things, so they put on masks and do great acting jobs to get through the day.
Miles: The Autobiography (1989)

Miles Davis. *Used by permission of the Schomburg Center for Research in Black Culture, The New York Public Library.*

191 He [his father] was always behind me 100% whatever I wanted
to do, and I believe that his confidence in me made me have
confidence in myself.

Miles: The Autobiography (1989)

❖ ❖ ❖

RUBY DEE
(Cleveland, Ohio, 1924–   )

*Actress, civil rights activist, and writer, Ruby Dee is more familiar to
the public for her theater roles. Her acting career has spanned more
than fifty years and has included radio, television, and films.*

192 Racism is a crusher. That we have survived this long in the face
of such concerted assaults on our psyches is a miracle. The question is, how do we let our children know what has happened to
us, and what continues to happen, without turning them into cyn-
ics and haters. We can't buy lies of the enemy, but we also have
to recognize our friends.

Washington Post (October 12, 1989)

193 The first function of art is to effect change. Nothing really exists
in isolation, and artists are providers of direction for change.

Washington Post (October 12, 1989)

194 I'm not a sociologist or a scientist. I can only address how I feel
and what I read. I think we hear so much about the negative
things, but I think as a species we're moving forward. I think
there's a great undercurrent of humanity in this country. That's
what makes it so extraordinary. But it's the aberrations that get
the headlines.

Washington Post (October 12, 1989)

195 There's hardly anything that is common to one group that isn't
common to any other.

Washington Post (October 12, 1989)

Ruby Dee. *Used by permission of the Schomburg Center for Research in Black Culture, The New York Public Library.*

196   We're doing a mad dance just trying to find out how to exist in this world. Racism just blinds us to the real problems that face us all.

I Dream a World (1989)

197   Everything is interdependent and things go together; night and day, youth and age. We have to understand and find out what the balance is, then know that life has its value in sharing what you've learned.

Modern Maturity (July 1994)

198   To begin to heal our communities, parents have to take charge. There's no substitute for somebody being in charge. Being an elder is more than sitting on a stoop with a pipe. Being an elder today is putting your ass on the line.

Essence (December 1994)

199   Freedom can only exist if it is bound to principles and anchored in economics.

Essence (December 1994)

❖ ❖ ❖

RON DELLUMS
(Oakland, California, 1935–   )

In 1993 Congressman Ron Dellums became chairman of the House Armed Services Committee, the first black to serve in this post. He was formerly the chair of the Congressional Black Caucus.

200   True peace entails more than the absence of war. It requires an unceasing effort to eliminate injustice, promote world peace and create a compassionate society—this is the legacy we must leave our children.

Address in celebration of his twenty years of service in
Congress (February 27, 1988)

Ron Dellums. *Used by permission of the Schomburg Center for Research in Black Culture, The New York Public Library.*

201   You don't understand the pain of being a black elected official carrying progressive ideas, when people in the media would render you invisible with the flick of the pen. What's welled up inside me is 20 years of pain, and if you ask any Black Caucus member, they feel exactly the same way.

Los Angeles Times (April 11, 1993)

202   I get up every day really humbled by the fact that there is so much that I don't know.

Los Angeles Times (April 11, 1993)

❖ ❖ ❖

MANU DIBANGO
(Douala, Cameroon, 1933–   )

During the 1970s and 1980s, saxophonist Manu Dibango was one of Europe's best-known African musicians and composers. Among his numerous honors and awards was the Chevalier des Arts et des Lettres from the French Ministry of Culture.

203   Today I still think sometimes that Africa has lost her pride. She has fallen into a deep sleep, and when she awakens, her various Princes Charming will look like ogres. The system devours its children and the rest of the planet watches the show, telling itself that though something's rotten in the black kingdom, there's no need to change what seems eternal. The misunderstanding is profound.

Three Kilos of Coffee (1994)

❖ ❖ ❖

DAVID DINKINS
(Trenton, New Jersey, 1927–)

David Dinkins was the first African-American elected mayor of New York City. He served from 1990 to 1994.

204 We must never forget the moral imperatives that count for more than money.
> Inaugural address for mayor, New York City (January 1990)

205 No matter how rich and powerful we become, we cannot be satisfied when so many children experience the sunset of opportunity at the very dawn of their existence.
> Inaugural address for mayor, New York City (January 1990)

❖ ❖ ❖

RITA DOVE
(Akron, Ohio, 1952–)

Poet, writer, educator, and the current U.S. poet laureate, Rita Dove is the youngest poet ever to hold this post of distinction at the Library of Congress.

206 Not that I'd want to forget being black, but I would love to walk through life without the anxiety of being prejudged and pigeonholed on the basis of my race.
> *Callaloo* (Spring 1991)

207 Poetry is language at its most distilled and most powerful. It's like a bouillon cube: you carry it around and then it nourishes you when you need it.
> *Washington Post* (May 19, 1993)

208 We are all individuals who may share in various groups certain things that make us feel that we have a community. But the in-

Rita Dove. *Used by permission of Rita Dove.*

dividual should never be obliterated or even blurred by that connection with the community.

Christian Science Monitor (May 26, 1993)

209   We tend to close off our souls and it just isn't cool to talk about it, to talk about having an interior life. If we don't acknowledge our own interior lives, we don't permit others to have them.

Washington Post (April 22, 1994)

❖ ❖ ❖

KATHERINE DUNHAM
(Joliet, Illinois, 1909–   )

Katherine Dunham is a world-renowned dancer who is credited with originating the concept of black dance theater. Also an anthropologist, Dunham was the first to study and incorporate elements of her ethnological and anthropological roots into dance.

210   You can get rhythmic action in an athlete, but it's the choreography that makes the dance.

I Dream a World (1989)

211   Each individual has within himself or herself the ability to change anything.

Crisis (October 1992)

212   I don't think of time as linear or even circular. But it's vital as long as you keep doing what you have to do.

Crisis (October 1992)

❖ ❖ ❖

MARIAN WRIGHT EDELMAN
(Bennettsville, South Carolina, 1939–   )

The founder and chairperson of the Children's Defense Fund, Marian Wright Edelman is a major advocate for American children of all ethnic groups. She is the author of Families in Peril: An Agenda for Social Change *(1987).*

213 Children cannot eat rhetoric and they cannot be sheltered by commissions. I don't want to see another commission that studies the needs of kids. We need to help them.

I Dream a World (1989)

214 In life the test and consequences come before the lessons.

Commencement Address, Howard University (May 12, 1990)

215 Don't assume a door is closed. Push on it.

Commencement Address, Howard University (May 12, 1990)

216 Don't be afraid of failing. It doesn't matter how many times you fall down. All that matters is how many times you keep getting up.

Commencement Address, Howard University (May 12, 1990)

217 Don't confuse wealth or fame with character.

Commencement Address, Howard University (May 12, 1990)

218 You are in charge of your own attitude.

The Measure of Our Success (1992)

219 One thing the country does not understand is that we don't have a child to waste.

New York Newsday (February 14, 1993)

220 While I never want to return to the old days of segregation ... I do want to return to the old spiritual roots, family and community bonds.

Ebony (November 1995)

221 Your life is filled with possibility. Reach high, look forward, and never give up. The world is waiting for you.

Introduction to *The Brownie's Book* (1996)

❖ ❖ ❖

JOYCELYN ELDERS
(Schaal, Arkansas, 1933–)

Joycelyn Elders is a physician of outstanding ability, energy, and commitment. In 1993 she became U.S. surgeon general but subsequently resigned because of her outspoken views.

222 There's so much to do. The train's on the track and it's coming towards us.

> *Washington Post* (February 16, 1993)

223 You can't be what you don't see.

> *New York Times* (January 30, 1994)

224 The confirmation process had very little to do with what kind of Surgeon General I would be. I felt it was more a mechanism to try to destroy me than anything else.

> *New York Times* (January 30, 1994)

225 Black women have always found that in the social order of things we're the least likely to be believed—by anyone.

> *New York Times* (January 30, 1994)

226 You've got to get people's attention before you can achieve change.

> *New York Times* (January 30, 1994)

❖ ❖ ❖

BUCHI EMECHETA
(Lagos, Nigeria, 1944–   )

Writer Buchi Emecheta earned a graduate degree in sociology from London University. She is the author of several novels, including Gwendolen *(1989) and* Head Above Water *(1994).*

227   Anger and disillusionment can make an animal of any dignitary.
The Rape of Shavi (1983)

228   Part of the celebration this night was to mark the end of a bitter and prolonged drought in which many people had died. They had no mongols or deformed people, because they got rid of them at birth, and those that lived by accident never survived that long. They had no means of artificially prolonging life. Every being had to be able to contribute something to the community in gratitude for being alive.
The Rape of Shavi (1983)

229   The women will have to fend for themselves in the future.
Africa Report (May–June 1990)

230   The English language does not belong to the English alone anymore. It is a world language. If one is lucky, it is a plus to be able to use it. In Nigeria we have 239 languages and English is still the lingua franca.
Africa Report (May–June 1990)

❖ ❖ ❖

EMMA S. ETUK
(Nigeria?, 1948–   )

Emma S. Etuk is a graduate of Ashland Theological Seminary in Ohio and author of Go Ye Out *(1985), a book on evangelism in Nigeria. She is widely known as a public speaker and is a member of the American Historical Association.*

231   We must define . . . what black destiny was or is. We must not leave others to do the job.

Destiny Is Not a Matter of Chance (1989)

232   For self-preservation to persist, there must necessarily be a vigilance, a watchful eye, "a voice in the wilderness," a willingness to protect and resist the oppressor. For black destiny to become realizable in a world of continuous anti-blackness, there must always be a perpetual vigilance on their part.

Destiny Is Not a Matter of Chance (1989)

❖ ❖ ❖

MYRLIE EVERS
(Vicksburg, Mississippi, 1933–   )

Myrlie Evers was the first black woman to hold the position of commissioner to the Los Angeles Board of Public Works. Widow of Medgar Evers, the slain civil rights leader, she continues to lead the fight for racial equality.

233   I see the challenges of the past with us today perhaps cloaked a little differently. This society is still dealing with racism. There is discrimination in education, in housing. I have faced discrimination for the color of my skin and because I am female. I have had jobs that have been the same jobs held by white males, and I have received 20% less pay. But we keep a-comin', as the song says—aware of ourselves and our strength. It is an exciting time to be alive.

Life (Spring 1988)

234   If one were to take a map of Mississippi and then take a list of people who were killed, beaten, lynched, raped, and who lost homes during the fifties and sixties and placed red pins for each incident, the state would be a red mass of suffering and pain.

I Dream a World (1989)

Myrlie Evers. *Used by permission of the Schomburg Center for Research in Black Culture, The New York Public Library.*

235 I have reached a point in my life where I understand the pain and the challenges, and my attitude is one of standing up with open arms to meet all of them.

I Dream a World (1989)

236 [Remark on being elected temporary chairperson of the NAACP:] We have to clean house. Where's my broom?

New York Newsday (February 19, 1995)

❖ ❖ ❖

LOUIS FARRAKHAN
(New York City, 1933–   )

The leader of the Nation of Islam, Louis Farrakhan has gained notoriety for his controversial remarks. He is a forceful presence on the African-American political landscape.

237 If men refuse to change the practice of reality to make the dream a reality and keep on sleeping on reality, hoping for a doctor, this generation will pass and another will come and they'll face the same problems that we faced.

Black Scholar (January–February 1979)

238 I can do nothing by myself and of myself, but together we can accomplish much.

Black Scholar (January–February 1979)

239 How can a man be late when his wisdom is on time?

Black Scholar (January–February 1979)

240 The first enemy you've got to confront is yourself. And you've got to confront that enemy where he's lurking in the higher regions of your mind, in your intelligence, in your so-called intelligence, right along with your knowledge.

Black Scholar (January–February 1979)

241   How in hell are we going to have a strong nation if we men can't cope with our women because they're too heavy for us?

Black Scholar (January–February 1979)

242   Any black person who commands the love and the respect of the masses is feared by those who don't control that one.

Address, Morgan State University (October 30, 1983)

243   Those who mockingly call us equal know that you can never be made somebody's equal. Equality is something you have to qualify for and if you don't know what to expect from yourself you don't even have the basis to begin to qualify to be equal.

"What Is the Need for Black History,"
address, Princeton University (1984)

244   You cannot show self-respect in a vacuum. Self-respect comes from a knowledge of self which makes you see yourself as you are.

"What Is the Need for Black History,"
address, Princeton University (1984)

245   All the elements are here to make America beautiful. You've got the whole planet's people living inside of America. If these people who represent the totality of the human family could live together in peace then the whole world could live together in peace.

"What Is the Need for Black History,"
address, Princeton University (1984)

246   If you were free you would not need the truth, you would have it already, but some human beings are enslaved in the bondage of ignorance, then men and women who would dare to see men free must never be afraid of consequence.

Address, JFK Center, Washington, D.C. (July 22, 1985)

247   Truth is the root of the universe and its order, but there must always be someone or someones who are willing to sacrifice to tell it.

Address, JFK Center, Washington, D.C. (July 22, 1985)

248   There is no difficulty that man is faced with that man does not have the ability to overcome, if he will summon the strength of his being against that obstacle in the pathway of his progress.

> Address, Symphony Hall, Phoenix, Arizona (August 21, 1986)

249   There are many brilliant black people. All they need is a chance.

> *Washington Post* (March 1, 1990)

250   I cannot give license to rage. It is injustice that gives license to rage. The people don't need a leader to direct their rage, they know who they are enraged against.

> *Washington Post* (March 1, 1990)

251   I don't think we can depend on whites to do for us what we could and should do for ourselves.

> *Atlanta Journal* (April 28, 1990)

252   I have lived in this world for 60 years and I'm going to be a winner.

> *New York Amsterdam News* (January 27, 1994)

253   What I represent is black suffering.

> *New York Amsterdam News* (January 27, 1994)

254   White supremacy must die in order for humanity to live.

> Address, Million Man March, Washington, D.C. (October 16, 1995)

❖ ❖ ❖

ROBERTA FLACK
(Asheville, North Carolina, 1940–   )

Roberta Flack taught high school in the early 1960s. After singing locally, she eventually recorded her first album. She has since become a top-performing jazz artist.

255   Salvation is in the work.

> *Essence* (February 1989)

256   One of the great joys of love is *loving*. To be loved in return is the second part.

Essence (February 1989)

257   Everything you do as a black person in this country represents some struggle for survival, if not on your part, then on the part of someone very close to you, or not so very far away.

Essence (February 1989)

❖ ❖ ❖

GEORGE FOREMAN
(Marshall, Texas, 1949–   )

Boxer George Foreman compiled an impressive knockout record—forty-two in forty-seven professional fights—a feat even Joe Louis could not match. He is now a minister.

258   The most important thing is you've got to make sure that what's in you comes out. It's not what you say. Nobody's about what they say anyway. It's about what's inside them. People can look right through you like animals, and especially kids. People say "Uh, huh. I know what he's all about." They never pay much attention, they just laugh at the punch line.

Ebony Male (November 1993)

259   If you'd been in the places deep in my mind where I've been, I bet you'd laugh till they put a hose on you.

Esquire (February 1995)

260   Can't eat without exercise.

Esquire (February 1995)

261   [On writers:]It's not who you think you are. It's what they think you are. Actually, I love writers. I'm a thief of what they write about me. I use it.

Esquire (February 1995)

262   I'm happenin'.

Esquire (February 1995)

263 Fame ain't much. That's what I began to think when I watched one of my German Shepherds years ago—a $21,000 dog—chewing in the garbage.

Esquire (February 1995)

264 Life is like boxing. You've only got so many punches to throw, and you can only take so many.

By George (1995)

265 Life can end as quickly as a smile.

By George (1995)

266 It was my mother who loved me enough to beat fear into me, and loved me enough to push me into the world that was best for me.

By George (1995)

267 I know from experience that the marriage of mind and body makes the sum more powerful than the individual parts.

By George (1995)

❖ ❖ ❖

JOHN HOPE FRANKLIN
(Rentiesville, Oklahoma, 1915–   )

For more than fifty years, John Hope Franklin has been an academic scholar and social activist. He is the author of over a dozen books and has received more than ninety honorary degrees.

268 There is nothing inherently wrong with being aware of color as long as it is seen as making distinctions in a pleasant, superficial, and unimportant manner. It is only when character is attached to color, when ability is measured by color, when privilege is tied to color, and a whole galaxy of factors that spell the difference between success and failure in our society are tied to color—it is only when such considerations are attached to color that it

John Hope Franklin. *Used by permission of the Schomburg Center for Research in Black Culture, The New York Public Library.*

becomes a deadly, dreadful, denigrating factor among us all. It is when it is such a factor that we have two nations, black and white, separate, hostile, unequal.

The Color Line: Legacy for the 21st Century (1993)

269 We need to do everything possible to emphasize the positive qualities that all of us have, qualities which we have never utilized to the fullest but which we must utilize if we are to solve the problem of the color line in the twenty-first century.

The Color Line: Legacy for the 21st Century (1993)

270 We can never expect public schools to teach us as much about our history as we want to know. We can urge them, we can press them to teach more, but I think that much of this lies within us.

Emerge (March 1994)

271 There's still racism manifested almost everywhere in this country.

Emerge (March 1994)

272 You could fill the shelves of the library with all the trash that's been written about what blacks can't do. People have bought that and still buy it.

Emerge (March 1994)

273 Blacks ought to help themselves more and stop crying about what they don't get. It's true they don't get much, but stop crying about it and go on and get more.

Emerge (March 1994)

274 We are the only country in the Western World that acts crazy like we act with guns.

Emerge (March 1994)

275 Almost from the beginning our Constitution was a flawed document, protecting the institution of slavery as it did in so many different ways, and yet expecting the blessings of independence to be spread over everyone—including slaves. . . . It was clearly, unequivocally hypocritical.

Los Angeles Times (July 2, 1995)

276 Assimilation is freedom to move, to participate, to belong on your terms, not someone else's. It is a certain kind of comfort zone in which you function. I don't enjoy that comfort zone—not even in 1995.

Los Angeles Times (July 2, 1995)

❖ ❖ ❖

MORGAN FREEMAN
(Memphis, Tennessee, 1937–)

Morgan Freeman is a versatile actor who has performed in roles ranging from children's television to Shakespearian drama. Some of his best-known roles were in the award-winning movies Driving Miss Daisy *(1989) and* Glory *(1989).*

277 Some people feel insignificant out at sea. I feel the most insignificant, like I have wings. I fly like all the other sea birds.

Los Angeles Times (December 18, 1989)

278 I'm a Southerner. I was shaped and molded by the south, and I never got Northernized. I realized I was a Southerner because every time I went back home I'd slip into it very comfortably. I like it there. It's home.

About . . . Time (February 1995)

❖ ❖ ❖

LEONORA B. FULANI
(Chester, Pennsylvania, 1951–)

Leonora Fulani is a social activist and former chairwoman of the New Alliance party. She is internationally known as a practitioner of social therapy and has led training in social therapy at agencies, universities, and professional conferences. She is author of Poor Women of Color Do Great Therapy *(1988).*

279 Those in control have spent billions of dollars and trillions of conniving hours destroying grass roots movements, leaders and peoples. For they are aware that the development of a real sense of community, of history, and of solidarity is a profound threat to their exploitative system of rule.

Poor Women of Color Do Great Therapy (1988)

280 Anyone can have positions. Those taken by the professional politicians are largely based on the dictates of the corporate political action committees that bankroll them and at election time, by what their poll takers say is currently "selling" among the electorate.

People's Planks (December 26, 1991)

❖ ❖ ❖

HENRY LOUIS GATES, JR.
(Keyser, West Virginia, 1950–   )

Literary scholar, professor, and critic, Henry Louis Gates, Jr., has won acclaim for his critical essays on black literature. He is the author of several books and is in demand as a lecturer throughout the United States.

281 We are the keepers of the black literary tradition. No matter what theories we seem to embrace, we have more in common with each other than we do with any other critic of any other literature.

Figures in Black (1987)

282 There's no point in trying to whitewash a multifarious cultural heritage, pretending it's a monolith of virtue. Like all cultures, black culture consists not only of the best that has been thought and said, but the worst as well. And unless you come to grips with that, you'll be caught in the specious one-dimensional logic of the "positive image" "negative image" opposition. And that's no way to do cultural criticism.

Callaloo (Spring 1991)

Henry Louis Gates, Jr. *Used by permission of Henry Louis Gates, Jr.*

283   This notion of calling a regional Anglo-American culture the world's only great culture was a mechanism of social, economic and political control. We have to expose that, critique it and move on, because it's a new world. We can either be rooted in the 19th century or we can blast off to a whole new millennium.

Time (April 22, 1991)

284   What I'm calling humanism starts not with the possession of identity, but with the capacity to *identify with*. It asks what we have in common with others, while acknowledging the diversity among ourselves. It is about the promise of a shared humanity.

New York Times (March 27, 1994)

❖ ❖ ❖

HAILE GERIMA
(Gondar, Ethiopia, 1946–   )

Playwright and filmmaker, Haile Gerima came to the United States in 1967, first to Chicago and then to the University of California at Los Angeles. There he wrote plays and later took up filmmaking. One of his most widely acclaimed films is Sankofa *(1993).*

285   As kids we tried to act out things we had seen in the movies. We used to play cowboys and Indians in the mountains around Gondar. . . . Even in Tarzan movies, whenever Africans sneaked up behind Tarzan we would scream our heads off trying to warn him that "they" were coming! It was the politically and psychologically damaging exploitation of my very being.

Framework (Spring 1978)

286   My father was an orthodox priest, a teacher, a historian and a playwright. He wrote plays of resistance to mobilize people during the Italian invasion of Ethiopia. He then joined the nationalist movement that brought him in direct conflict with his own church which collaborated with the Italians. Thus, from then on he de-

nounced religion. My mother was educated by Catholic mission-
aries, and so she raised us in the Catholic faith.

Journal of the University Film and Video Association (Spring 1983)

287   When you sit silently and pensively, reflecting in moments of
introspection in your mind, you are capable of receiving information, like telegrams from the soul of the past.

Atlanta Tribune (September 15, 1994)

❖ ❖ ❖

PAULA GIDDINGS
(Yonkers, New York, 1947–   )

*Paula Giddings is a journalist, editor, and author. She uses her writing
to present, analyze, and illuminate information and ideas in order to
create change in society.*

288   Black women could understand the relationship between racism
and sexism because they had to strive against both. In doing so
they became the linchpin between two of the most important social reform movements in American history, the struggles for
Black rights and women's rights. In the course of defying the
imposed limitations on race and sex, they loosened the chains
around both.

When and Where I Enter (1985)

❖ ❖ ❖

GILBERTO GIL
(Salvador, Brazil, 1943–   )

*Gilberto Gil, a highly popular international musician, has blended a
cross-cultural mix of jazz and pop. He has produced numerous best-
selling recordings.*

289   The great steamroller of black culture and its contribution is our
carnival spirit. It is we who taught Brazil how to celebrate. We

taught the country how to belly-laugh, how to turn cartwheels, how to make a colorful banner out of a shred of cloth, how to turn a stick into a musical instrument.

World Press Review (May 1988)

❖ ❖ ❖

BERTHA KNOX GILKEY
(Sanfran, Arkansas, 1949–   )

Bertha Knox Gilkey is perhaps the nation's premier tenants' rights advocate. As president of the Cochran Tenant Management Corp. and an activist for welfare and tenants' rights, she organized the tenants of a deteriorated housing complex, Cochran Gardens, St. Louis, Missouri, to regain control of their community.

290   There is big money in poor folks. There's millions of people that benefit. They eat because I'm poor. They never want to eliminate poverty. They just want to control it. The day they eliminate poverty, they go out of business.

I Dream a World (1989)

❖ ❖ ❖

CAROLE GIST
(Detroit, Michigan, 1970?–   )

In 1990 Carole Gist became the first black woman to capture the title of Miss USA.

291   I do believe that some of the negative things in my childhood are positive for me now. They made me what I am today. I had not the happiest of upbringings, but you don't have to become a statistic just because you grew up in a broken home.

Jet (March 26, 1990)

292   It's nice to be first at something. I like being the one to help lay the groundwork.

Jet (March 26, 1990)

❖ ❖ ❖

DANNY GLOVER
(San Francisco, California, 1947–   )

Actor Danny Glover's career began on the stage, and later he made a successful transition to the screen. He has starred in top roles in The Color Purple *(1985),* To Sleep with Anger *(1990), and* Lethal Weapon *(1987), among others.*

293   My grandmother delivered half a county as midwife and raised other people's kids. She nurtured, and that's something our culture has lost sight of.

Vis à Vis (October 1991)

294   Even smiling at someone, I feel as if I'm doing something to make the world a better place. I'd be doing that even if I weren't an actor.

Vis à Vis (October 1991)

295   One of the incredible things about women is that they have the capacity to experience and to feel so much more. And that they are just so magnificent.

Playboy (September 1991)

296   You *have* to get beyond the fear.

New York Newsday (May 12, 1992)

❖ ❖ ❖

WHOOPI GOLDBERG
(New York City, 1949–   )

Comedienne, actress, and social activist, Whoopi Goldberg is familiar to film and television audiences. She has won many honors, including the Golden Globe Award, NAACP Image Award, and an Academy Award nomination for The Color Purple *(1985) and an Academy Award for* Ghost *(1991).*

297 Tenacity is everything.

Au Courant (October 8, 1990)

298 There ain't no joy in a high—none. You *think* there's a joy in a high because it feels good temporarily. But it feels good less and less often, so you've got to do it more and more often. It ain't your friend.

Ebony (March 1991)

299 The greatest thing I ever was able to do was give a welfare check back.

Ebony (March 1991)

300 If there wasn't something called acting they would probably hospitalize people like me. The giddiness and the joy of life is the moving and grooving, the exploration.

Ebony (March 1991)

301 I believe I'm here for a reason. And I think a little bit of the reason is to throw little torches out to the next step to lead people through the dark. When you're kind to someone in trouble you hope they'll remember to be kind to someone else.

Ebony (March 1991)

302 I think that it's important for me as a humanist to really be in touch with the things that affect us as human beings.

Preview (September 13–19, 1992)

303 If you're alone with the knowledge that you are a viable, good human being, regardless of your circumstance, it makes it a lot easier to carry the force with you, to go beyond it.

Interview (June 1992)

304 What I am is a humanist before anything—before I'm a Jew, before I'm black, before I'm a woman. And my beliefs are for the human race—they don't exclude anyone.

Interview (June 1992)

❖ ❖ ❖

JEWELLE GOMEZ
(Boston, Massachusetts, 1948–   )

Jewelle Gomez is an activist, teacher, arts administrator, and literary critic.

305   Too many black women come to believe that the violence suffered at the hands of the men in their lives is simply intrinsic to the relationship rather than just another form of violence exercised by someone who views himself as authority, no matter how limited the scope of his domain.

Forty-three Septembers (1993)

306   My sense of myself grows explicitly out of what it is to have a special "American" persona. There is a combination of elements that make me individual: African-American, Ioway, Wampanoag, Bostonian, lesbian, welfare-raised, artist, activist.

Forty-three Septembers (1993)

❖ ❖ ❖

BERRY GORDY, JR.
(Detroit, Michigan, 1929–   )

Berry Gordy, Jr., recording industry executive, and entrepreneur, established Motown Records in 1959. During the 1960s and 1970s the Detroit-based record label grew into a full-fledged entertainment corporation. Among Gordy's many honors is membership in the Rock and Roll Hall of Fame.

307   If somebody told me today, "Okay, you're gonna go into business, and you've gotta make a profit every year for the first five years or you'll be out of business," I'd say that's not a good gamble. But that's what we did. Motown was a freak.

Rolling Stone (August 23, 1990)

308   He [Smokey Robinson] had a purity about him, and he had a feeling of great thankfulness. Even as I rejected every song, he got stronger, and that's hard. That's the mark of a real kind of winner.

Rolling Stone (August 23, 1990)

309 All people have the same wants and likes and dislikes. That's always been my thing—trying to get the thread between all people.

Rolling Stone (August 23, 1990)

310 You can read 25 positive things about yourself and feel great, and then you hear one negative thing that's a lie, and it bothers the hell out of you.

Los Angeles Times (December 1, 1994)

311 Less than one percent of the people in the world reach their full potential—and the reason is they take their focus off what they were doing.

Los Angeles Times (December 1, 1994)

312 Motown was a world unto itself—and the sound was a benefit of that kind of world.

Los Angeles Times (December 1, 1994)

313 The first song I tried to sell was a song I wrote for Doris Day, a white-sounding song for a white girl. So I sold out my white roots when I changed to black music.

Playboy (August 1995)

314 Stardom affects people in many different ways, and some can make it through the vicious circle. Others get caught in drugs, some go mad with power, some forget who their friends are, some forget who they are.

Playboy (August 1995)

315 I learned ages ago that money cannot make you happy. And I realized that unless you have money, you can't make a statement.

Playboy (August 1995)

316 To exploit is not necessarily bad. To make use of someone's talent in a positive way benefits everyone.

Playboy (August 1995)

317   Not all rap music is about whores and bitches. . . . Much of rap is about the conditions under which rappers live. It's a language they have developed to describe what they go through. They're putting it on record for everyone to hear.

Playboy (August 1995)

318   Artistic freedom is important, but if you think something is damaging to society, that's something else. We have a responsibility not to hurt people willfully. And we must remember that creative people are very powerful.

Playboy (August 1995)

❖ ❖ ❖

LOUIS GOSSETT, JR.
(Brooklyn, New York, 1936–   )

Louis Gossett is an actor known for the depth and diversity of his roles. He has performed in more than sixty Broadway and off-Broadway productions, a score of feature films, television movies, and miniseries.

319   There's something spiritual in the whole process of fruit growing, something close to nature, something about God. I don't care how many Oscars or Emmys or prizes you've won or how much money you have, you live with trees and I promise it will help you keep your feet on the ground.

GQ: Gentleman's Quarterly (December 1988)

320   Racial prejudice was something we transcended. I was formed with the idea there was nothing I couldn't do because I was black. The only thing my parents were worried about was that I would be heartbroken when I found out later how things were when I left the community. But the community insulated us and prepared us for what was right in mankind. Today, it still sits inside of

Louis Gossett, Jr. *Used by permission of the Schomburg Center for Research in Black Culture, The New York Public Library.*

me. The melting pot upbringing has propelled me across this world. There are injustices, but I believe that man's basic humanity to man is much stronger than his inhumanity.

New York Newsday (June 3, 1990)

❖ ❖ ❖

EARL GRAVES
(Brooklyn, New York, 1935–   )

Publisher and corporate executive officer Earl Graves is a highly respected and nationally known authority on black business development. He is the founder and publisher of Black Enterprise *magazine.*

321   We cannot forget the past until the past is over for everyone who happens to be black in America.

Commencement address, Howard University (May 13, 1989)

322   These final barriers to equal economic opportunity are based on the diabolic part of human nature which seems to make it necessary for one group of people to feel superior to—and at the same time threatened by—another. It is this base, parochial quality of human nature that is not only the cause of racism, but also has caused most of the wars in human history.

Commencement address, Howard University (May 13, 1989)

❖ ❖ ❖

LANI GUINIER
(New York City, 1950–   )

Activist, lawyer, educator, and writer, Lani Guinier is noted for her commitment to racial equality. Her moment in the history of American government arose when President Bill Clinton nominated her to the Justice Department's top civil rights post in 1993 and later withdrew the nomination because of her views on civil rights.

323   We are survivors, not victims, and we have to take a stand or

Earl Graves. *Used by permission of the Schomburg Center for Research in Black Culture, The New York Public Library.*

take a step or make a statement that allows us to move from being the victim of other people's decisions to the architect of our own well-being and that of our community and country.

Essence (October 1994)

324   It's more helpful to talk to people about things they can change and about things they can do to make the lives of the people around them better.

Essence (October 1994)

325   Democracy in a heterogeneous society is incompatible with rule by a racial monopoly of any color.

The Tyranny of the Majority (1994)

326   I am a democratic idealist who believes that politics need not be forever seen as I win, you lose, a dynamic in which some people are permanent monopoly winners and others are permanent excluded losers.

Press conference, Justice Department, Washington, D.C. (June 4, 1994)

❖ ❖ ❖

BRYANT GUMBEL
(New Orleans, Louisiana, 1948–   )

Bryant Gumbel began his career as a sportswriter, assuming his broadcasting career in 1972. He later became a regular television sportscaster on the Today Show *and was named co-anchor in 1981, the first black to hold that position.*

327   We're all challenged by a loss of things in our life that to a great degree are beyond our control. This is a game that's totally you, and when you screw it up, there's absolutely no one to blame.

Mirabella (February 1993)

328   There are very few perceptions in this country that are not tinged by race.

Mirabella (February 1993)

329   I think for a number of people, the idea of a secure, confident

male who is black is disturbing, and possibly, unnerving.

Mirabella (February 1993)

❖ ❖ ❖

ARSENIO HALL
(Cleveland, Ohio, 1956–)

In 1989 Arsenio Hall became host of a syndicated talk show that quickly became popular with the young, hip audience. He parlayed the show, which ran over five years, into a slot of top late-night entertainment. Hall plans to develop sitcom material for young comics.

330   When you broke a window in my neighborhood it was never replaced with another window, always masking tape and dry cleaner's plastic bags. I lived in the house on the corner of the block that they *didn't* tear down. Sometimes, I think the most painful elements of my life have created my talkshow.

Voice (May 23, 1989)

331   I was a very lonely kid.

Voice (May 23, 1989)

332   A lot of people think you get into the class clown thing because you're the funniest guy in the class, or whatever. I was who I was because at home there was no one to laugh at me, there was no one to play with me.

Voice (May 23, 1989)

333   I'm a real person—life's a bitch. I live to put a smile on your face and make your life a little bit better. This is a very tough world we live in.

Voice (May 23, 1989)

334   There's a subconscious racism that's been driven on blacks so hard that it's become part of their attitude about everything. But

you cannot become part of the oppression. I want to hear black people say, "I can do anything."

Rolling Stone (November 1, 1989)

335 It's so hard to get me mad or shake me up out there because I am in my world. I am smiling and happy to be here. You need a crane to pull my top lip down over my gums.

Us (October 1990)

336 As a Black man I see myself making an attempt to not only make people laugh, but to make history.

Ebony (December 1990)

337 The days of us keeping each other down, the days of us fighting each other and not understanding there is tremendous power in unity, are over.

Ebony (December 1990)

❖ ❖ ❖

CHARLES V. HAMILTON
(Muskogee, Oklahoma, 1927–   )

Charles Hamilton has taught at several universities and published widely. He is author of Adam Clayton Powell, Jr.: The Political Biography of an American Dilemma *(1991).*

338 Without historical perspective you can only politicize—you can't teach.

Columbia (Summer 1992)

SHAHEEN HAQUE
(London, England, 1948–)

Shaheen Haque is an architect whose work centers on developing non-Eurocentric architectural practices.

339 As a black woman architect I believe that architecture is also forged by the politics of space. It is essentially about the power structures that fund the white middle class architect who makes up the body of the profession. They create the physical environment in which we live and reinforce through their designs their problematic definition of women, Black people and the working class. . . . Inevitably the buildings they produce reflect a limited response to the arts and to the social life of the people they design for and, by doing so, limit the life choices of the Black and working class.

Dissertation (1988)

❖ ❖ ❖

BARBARA C. HARRIS
(Philadelphia, Pennsylvania, 1931–)

On February 11, 1989, Barbara Harris became the first woman to be consecrated a bishop in the Anglican communion.

340 I am not accustomed to quiet. I am used to boom boxes and people talking in the street.

Episcopalian (February 1990)

341 I think older people are more open to change than we give them credit for being. . . . You can't fool them. If I were not genuine then I think they would spot me as a phony. I would never try to fool them.

Episcopalian (February 1990)

❖ ❖ ❖

ISAAC HAYES
(Covington, Tennessee, 1943–   )

Isaac Hayes was one of the top rhythm-and-blues recording artists during the late 1960s and early 1970s. After a twenty-four-year hiatus, he recently returned to the music scene.

342   We never had Black History Month when I was in an all-black school. It wasn't until later that I finally realized that we did have a history beyond the European perspective. . . . For years we were so racially divided, and it's not going to get any better until we really learn about ourselves and other ethnicities learn about us, too.

Interview (May 1995)

343   That's what I try to tell my Afro-American brothers and sisters: Embrace your blues. There's a great deal of responsibility that goes with music, because it moves people. It's universal. It gets everybody. When you have that kind of power, art is the purest form of communication. We have to be very careful how we use that responsibility and do it in a positive way.

Interview (May 1995)

344   It's our time.

New York Newsday (May 30, 1995)

345   I'm a soul brother, I'm a soul man.

Washington Post (September 24, 1995)

346   [Song title:] Hyperbolicsyllabicsesquedalymistic.

Washington Post (September 24, 1995)

Isaac Hayes. *Used by permission of the Schomburg Center for Research in Black Culture, The New York Public Library.*

BESSIE HEAD
(Pietermaritzburg, South Africa, 1937–1986)

Bessie Head is one of Africa's best-known women writers. She was sent to a foster family at the age of thirteen and mission school before training as a teacher. She was a permanent exile in Botswana. Her works include Maru *(1971),* A Question of Power *(1973),* The Collector of Treasures *(1977), and* A Betwitched Crossroad *(1984).*

347   Poverty has a home in Africa—like a quiet second skin. It may be the only place on earth where it is worn with an unconscious dignity.

Village People (1967)

348   It is hard to imagine a heaven where the Pope officiates, because so many people would have to be excluded.

African Religions (1969)

349   Each human society is a narrow world, trapped to death in paltry evils and jealousies, and for people to know that there are thoughts and generosities wider and freer than their own can be an enrichment to their lives.

Epilogue: An African Story (1972)

350   People who have suffered from the wanton cruelty of others prefer the truth at all times, no matter what it might cost them.

A Question of Power (1973)

351   A heaven had been planned directly around the hearts of men and as, bit by bit its plan unfolded they called it so many names: freedom of thought, social consciousness, protest, human rights, exploration, moral orders, principles and a thousand and one additions for the continual expansion and evolution of the human soul.

A Question of Power (1973)

352   Love is so powerful, it's like unseen flowers under your feet as you walk.

A Question of Power (1973)

353 God is people. There's nothing up there. It's all down here.

A Question of Power (1973)

354 I need a quiet backwater and a sense of living as though I am barely alive on the earth, treading a small careful pathway through life.

Notes from a Quiet Backwater II (1982)

355 I have not a single known relative on earth, no long and ancient family tree to refer to, no links with heredity or a sense of having inherited a temperament, a certain emotional stability or the shape of a fingernail from a grandmother.

A Woman Alone: Autobiographical Writings (1986)

❖ ❖ ❖

ANITA HILL
(Morris, Oklahoma, 1956–   )

Lawyer, social activist, and educator, Anita Hill gained notoriety when she brought charges of sexual harassment against a former employer, Clarence Thomas. She went public during his confirmation hearings on his nomination to the U.S. Supreme Court.

356 It would have been more comfortable to remain silent. It took no initiative to inform anyone. But when I was asked by a representative of this committee to report my experience, I felt that I had to tell the truth. I could not keep silent.

Statement to the Senate Judiciary Committee (October 11, 1991)

❖ ❖ ❖

GRANT HILL
(Dallas, Texas, 1972–   )

Grant Hill was co-winner of the National Basketball Association's 1994 Rookie of the Year Award and the league's only rookie ever to finish first in All-Star voting.

357   I like bookstores, and not because I like to read. People leave you alone in bookstores.

Esquire (February 1995)

358   I was brought up to believe the important thing was not how much money you want but how much money you save.

Esquire (February 1995)

359   I hate losing.

Esquire (February 1995)

360   People may only see one side of me—the dunking, the basketball playing—but my parents were real strict on me. If I didn't do well in the classroom I couldn't play. Period. They were big on education.

Interview (April 1995)

361   I'm not going to change who I am to please anybody.

GQ: Gentlemen's Quarterly (April 1995)

362   I don't have to do anything to prove my blackness.

GQ: Gentlemen's Quarterly (April 1995)

❖ ❖ ❖

GREGORY HINES
(New York City, 1946–   )

Gregory Hines is a show business veteran who has appeared in films, on stage and television, and in nightclubs. He is best known for his dazzling performances as a tap dancer.

363   My father was a symbol for me of what a black man could stand for—and he still is. He has so much pride.

Parade (May 31, 1992)

364 The best entertainment speaks to the human condition in an honest way.

Parade (May 31, 1992)

365 Luck is opportunity meeting up with preparation, so you must prepare yourself to be lucky.

Parade (May 31, 1992)

366 I'm going to tap dance until I can't.

Parade (May 31, 1992)

367 I've been a black person for a long time. I've learned about how important it is to be aggressive if you're going to get what you want. You've got to keep going and make things happen.

New York Daily News (December 3, 1995)

368 When I'm tap dancing I sometimes feel like I'm in the ''zone'' that baseball and football players talk about. I feel endless ideas and emotions flowing out of me. I feel like I could dance forever. That's why I love to put my tap shoes on.

New York Daily News (December 3, 1995)

❖ ❖ ❖

MILT HINTON
(Vicksburg, Mississippi, 1910–   )

Milt Hinton, the dean of bass players, has experienced the jazz world firsthand for more than five decades. A member of Cab Calloway's band for over fifteen years, he has played with most of the jazz greats of this century, including Louis Armstrong, Count Basie, Duke Ellington, and Dizzy Gillespie.

369 I started playing the violin at 13 and from that point on, whenever something bad happened, I'd go off alone and play my music. It became my religion. It was my salvation and it sustained me.

Bass Line (1988)

370   I was pretty young when I realized the music involves more than just playing an instrument. Its really about cohesiveness and sharing. All my life I've felt obliged to try and teach anyone who would listen. I've always believed you don't truly know something yourself until you can take it from your mind and put it in someone else's.

Bass Line (1988)

371   It's nice to remind people about the dues that some of us paid in order to keep this thing going. Jazz is here because a whole group of people paid some hard dues.

(*New York Times* (June 23, 1990)

BELL HOOKS
(Hopkinsville, Kentucky, 1952–   )

bell hooks is a philosopher, feminist, social critic, and prolific writer.

372   It has been a political struggle for me to hold to the belief that there is much we—black people—must speak about that is private that must be openly shared, if we are to heal our wounds (hurts caused by domination and exploitation and oppression), if we are to recover and realize ourselves.

Talking Back (1989)

373   There are times when so much talk, or writing, so many ideas seem to stand in the way to block the awareness that for the oppressed, the exploited, the dominated, domination is not just a subject for radical discourse, of books. It is about pain—the pain of hunger, the pain of overwork, the pain of degradation and dehumanization, the pain of loneliness, the pain of loss, the pain of isolation, the pain of exile—spiritual and physical.

Talking Back (1989)

374 [On the black woman:] To her, black people make the most passionate music. She knows that there is no such thing as natural rhythm. She knows it is the intensity of feeling, the constant knowing that death is real and a possibility that makes the music what it is. She knows that it is the transformation of suffering and sorrow into sounds that bears witness to the black past. In her dreams she has seen the alchemist turning lead into gold.

Black Is a Woman's Color (1989)

375 Without an ongoing active movement to end white supremacy, without ongoing black liberation struggle, no social environment can exist in the U.S. that truly supports integration.

Overcoming White Supremacy: A Comment (1991)

376 What might black men do for themselves and for black people if they were not socialized by white supremacist capitalist patriarchy to focus their attention on their penises. . . . Such confused men have little time or insight for resistance to struggle.

Reconstructing Black Masculinity, Black Looks (1992)

377 Within a white supremacist culture, to be without documentation is to be without a legitimate history. In the culture of forgetfulness, memory alone has no meaning.

Revolutionary Renegades, Black Looks (1992)

378 If I were really asked to define myself, I wouldn't start with race; I wouldn't start with blackness; I wouldn't start with gender; I wouldn't start with feminism. I would start with stripping down to what fundamentally informs my life, which is that I'm a seeker on the path. I think of feminism, and I think of anti-racist struggles as part of it. But where I stand spiritually is, steadfastly, on a path about love.

Tricycle: The Buddhist Review (Fall 1992)

379 In real love, real union, or communion there are no rules.

Tricycle: The Buddhist Review (Fall 1992)

380   To be capable of love one has to be capable of suffering and of acknowledging one's suffering. We all suffer, rich and poor. The fact is that when people have material privilege at the enormous expense of others, they live in a state of terror as well. It's the unease of having to protect your gain.

Tricycle: The Buddhist Review (Fall 1992)

381   There is no change without contemplation.

Tricycle: The Buddhist Review (Fall 1992)

382   Self-love for black people isn't about changing our hairdo to a natural for a year and then saying "Oh, I'm free." It's a constant practice of self-love.

Essence (May 1995)

❖ ❖ ❖

BENJAMIN HOOKS
(Memphis, Tennessee, 1925–   )

Benjamin Hooks was active during the 1960s civil rights struggle and became the first black appointee to the Federal Communications Commission. For fifteen years he presided over the National Association for the Advancement of Colored People.

383   With hard work, commitment and faith, there is very little that men and women of good faith cannot accomplish.

Crisis (January 1989)

❖ ❖ ❖

LENA HORNE
(Brooklyn, New York, 1917–   )

Lena Horne, an incomparable entertainer, has performed on the stage, in films, and on television, and she has many recordings to her credit. Among her awards are the Ebony Lifetime Achievement Award and two Grammies.

384 Don't be afraid to feel as angry or as loving as you can, because when you feel nothing, it's just death.

I Dream a World (1989)

385 People were rapping in my grandfather's day. They called it signifying.

USA Today (May 20, 1994)

386 I never forgot for a moment who I was or where I came from. It was the acceptance of my people that matters most to me.

Los Angeles Times (May 31, 1994)

❖ ❖ ❖

WHITNEY HOUSTON
(East Orange, New Jersey, 1963–   )

Whitney Houston began her singing career with the highest-selling solo album in history and went on to sell millions of copies of her subsequent releases. She has won numerous music awards and has also starred in films.

387 Racism doesn't play a part in my life. The heavy part about racism for me is that it's just a word we use today. At one time there was segregation. At one time it was prejudice. And now it's just racism. Doesn't it mean one group of people discriminating against another group of people? Well, I've seen that happen in every country. . . . A lot of brothers and sisters have fought the fight so that we can stand here today and be judged not by skin color but by the content of our character.

Playboy (May 1991)

388   There's a certain rage and anger about being black in this country. But now we must learn how to fight it. . . . It's about dealing with white people with our minds, because that's how they've been dealing with us.

Playboy (May 1991)

❖ ❖ ❖

MILDRED HOWARD
(Berkeley, California, 1945–   )

Artist Mildred Howard has been a social activist in the San Francisco Bay Area for many years. She is not only a maker of powerful images but also one of the creators of Bay Area culture. She has exhibited her artwork extensively throughout the United States.

389   I think that if we continue to separate ourselves as black or white artists then we separate ourselves from a larger audience. I just happen to be black, which I feel is an attribute, but it shouldn't be an issue. Art has to be more universal.

Connecting Conversations (1988)

❖ ❖ ❖

CHARLAYNE HUNTER-GAULT
(Due West, South Carolina, 1942–   )

Charlayne Hunter-Gault was one of the first African-American students to attend the University of Georgia in 1961. Over the years she has received several journalism awards.

390 Whatever I have faced as a woman is probably a lot more subtle than what I have faced as a black person.

I Dream a World (1989)

391 If people are informed they will do the right thing. It's when they are not informed that they become hostages to prejudice.

I Dream a World (1989)

392 When people at the top exercise aggressive leadership and will, even when they don't work miracles, they set a tone and create an atmosphere that makes things happen.

In Our Place (1992)

393 I do not believe we can function as a secure society if we are not at peace with ourselves.

In Our Place (1992)

❖ ❖ ❖

ICE-T (Tracy Morrow)
(Newark, New Jersey, 1958–   )

Ice-T has had great success as a rapper and recording artist, and has expanded into acting. As a social commentator, he continues his assault on racism and mainstream sensibilities.

394 If you're not into neutralization of race, you're in trouble.

Washington Post (July 17, 1991)

395 Everybody in the ghetto aspires to get out. Nobody with sense wants to live there with rats, roaches, crime and drugs.

Los Angeles Times (March 21, 1993)

396 Because of his upbringing, the ghetto black man has this built-in mechanism he's trying to control. You shouldn't push him toward the edge. Sometimes you're dealing with people who are so frustrated, they are on the brink of insanity.

Playboy (February 1994)

❖ ❖ ❖

IMAN
(Mogadishu, Somalia, 1955–)

Iman, one of the highest-paid models in the world, is also an actress and social activist in Somalia.

397 I've proven I can break the rules. . . . It's not about confidence. It's about being exact. You've got to know what you can do and what you cannot.

Essence (January 1988)

❖ ❖ ❖

FRANCES JACKSON
(Baltimore, Maryland, 1929–)

Frances Jackson is a gospel singer and conductor.

398 I am unashamedly Christian and unapologetically black. I'm the moan and groan of the black mother on a boat coming to America in chains. I'm the sound of the cotton and the house slave crying "Oh, Lord How Long." . . . I am gospel music. I am the black experience.

Voices of Traditions: African-American Gospel Music (1989)

❖ ❖ ❖

JANET JACKSON
(Gary, Indiana, 1966–   )

Janet Jackson made her mark as a young television actress; by the beginning of the 1990s, she had established herself as a singer on the way to superstar status. She has recorded several platinum albums and won numerous music awards.

399   [On her album "Rhythm Nation":] Even if only one person out of all those who listen to the album makes a change, that's an accomplishment.

Ebony (February 1990)

400   I don't believe in luck. It's hard work and not forgetting your dream—and going after it. It's about still having hunger in your heart.

Ebony (September 1993)

401   A lot of people harp on "this is what they did to us" and "they did that to us" talking about the white man. Okay, fine. We know everything that has happened to us. Now it's time to move on.

Ebony (September 1993)

402   [Most valuable lesson learned from her parents:] Always follow your heart, and never forget where you came from. Always extend your hand to help others.

Ebony (September 1993)

❖ ❖ ❖

JESSE JACKSON
(Greenville, South Carolina, 1941–   )

As founder and president of the National Rainbow Coalition, Jesse Jackson has firmly established himself as a dynamic force for social and political action, both nationally and internationally.

403   Dreamers are killed early. Leadership involves bearing a cross.

Crisis (October 1995)

404   The black community needs those who will shake trees; who will disturb the comfortable and comfort the disturbed. I am a tree shaker.

Crisis (October 1995)

405   Those who do the tree shaking, those who take the risk and go counter to culture and face loss of limb, of life or jail, the beneficiaries have an obligation to reinvest. Honeybees have that much sense.

Crisis (October 1995)

406   We are all free to sacrifice.

Crisis (October 1995)

407   Often those in power divide the have-nots. They tell one group of have-nots that they have not because of another group of have-nots. Don't fall prey to demagogues who use hate, hurt and hostility as weapons. We should turn to each other, not on each other.

USA Weekend (November 24–26, 1995)

408   Slavery and segregation were government plans. The government cannot wash its hands. It can't step away from its responsibility to correct its errors.

USA Weekend (November 24–26, 1995)

409   The challenge is to turn midnights into days, pain into power. If you're swimming, and there's a stiff wind and a vicious storm coming, you can't stop swimming and explain the storm away. You've got to keep kicking.

USA Weekend (November 24–26, 1995)

410   If you give up, you cannot win with honor when you die without dignity. The evidence is when we fight back against over-climbing odds, we win. We lose many ball games now, not because of a superior pitcher, because we don't show up with the bat.

EM: Ebony Male (December 1995)

411 We have unused political power, enough to determine the course of the country.

EM: Ebony Male (December 1995)

412 As I look back on the struggles and triumphs of my mother and that long line of black men and women who survived slavery and segregation and armies of doubting Thomases, I am grateful to the Lord for letting me see the glory of the coming of a new day, and I am persuaded, once again, that God and history are not through with us yet.

Ebony (December 1995)

❖ ❖ ❖

MICHAEL JACKSON
(Gary, Indiana, 1958–   )

Michael Jackson is one of the great entertainers of the era.

413 I am a perfectionist by nature. I like things to be the best they can be. I want people to hear or watch something I've done and feel that I've given it everything I've got. I feel I owe an audience that courtesy.

Moonwalk (1988)

414 What one wishes is to be touched by the truth and to be able to interpret that truth so that one may use what one is feeling and experiencing, be it despair or joy, in a way that will add meaning to one's life and will hopefully touch others as well. This is art in its highest form. Those moments of enlightenment are what I continue to live for.

Moonwalk (1988)

415 Trusting yourself begins by recognizing that it's okay to be afraid. Having fear is not the problem, because everyone feels anxious and insecure sometimes. The problem is not being honest enough to admit your fear. Whenever I accept my own doubt and insecurity I'm more open to other people. The deeper I go into myself, the stronger I become, because I realize that my real self is much bigger than any fear.

Dancing the Dream (1992)

416 Love is a funny thing to describe. It's so easy to feel and yet so slippery to talk about. It's like a bar of soap in the bathtub—you have it in your hand until you hold on too tight.

Dancing the Dream (1992)

417 People ask me how I make music. I tell them I just step into it. It's like stepping into a river and joining the flow. Every moment in the river has its song. So I stay in the moment and listen.

Dancing the Dream (1992)

418 We've been treating Mother Earth the way some people treat a rental apartment. Just trash it and move on.

Dancing the Dream (1992)

419 My goal in life is to give to the world what I was lucky to receive: the ecstasy of divine union through my music and dance.

In His Own Words (1993)

420 I hate to take credit for the songs I've written. I feel that some- where, someplace, it's been done and I'm just a courier bringing it out into the world.

In His Own Words (1993)

421 I happen to be color blind. I don't hire color, I hire competence. The individual can be of any race or creed as long as I get the best. Racism is not my motto. One day I strongly expect every color to love as one family.

In His Own Words (1993)

422 Once when we were coming back from Africa in total darkness, we were way up and there were so many shooting stars I thought they were going to hit the plane. When you're up there where there's no smog, you almost don't see any darkness. You almost don't see any black for all the stars.

In His Own Words (1993)

❖ ❖ ❖

JUDITH JAMISON
(Decatur, Alabama, 1956–)

Judith Jamison is a former lead dancer with the Alvin Ailey American Dance Theater. She became its artistic director in 1989.

423   The black issue is one thing that I don't want to take up because it forces people into pigeonholes. I like the idea of responding to all ethnic backgrounds—not focusing on a single one.

Los Angeles Times (October 22, 1989)

424   I am a sum total of all our influences. And it's out of that that I discover my art. I pray for the day when only our humanity and talent—not our skin color—identify us.

Los Angeles Times (October 22, 1989)

425   If anyone loses even a single right, we risk losing them all.

Los Angeles Times (May 8, 1990)

426   Our house was built with bricks, heated with coal and filled with love.

In the Spirit (1993)

427   Everything is linked. Movement comes from the center of our body. Spiritually it comes from the light that is inside. It's supposed to emanate from the core of your being. If your core is in your kneecap, have it emanate from there.

In the Spirit (1993)

428   I remember always the need to know myself, because if I avoid knowing who I am deep inside then I can't express what I have to say through the talent that I have.

In the Spirit (1993)

429   Learn the craft of knowing how to open your heart and how to turn on your creativity. There's a light inside of you.

In the Spirit (1993)

430   Dance from the top of your head to the bottom of your feet. There is no step that is not justified. Even when you are stationary, you must be moving and alive. Even static sculpture has movement. You may be standing still but you are moving. Energy is coming out. And for that you have to be alert. Be clear—it is the only way to bring forth the honesty in movement.

In the Spirit (1993)

MAE C. JEMISON
(Decatur, Alabama, 1956–   )

Mae Jemison is the first African-American female astronaut.

431   It's important not only for a little black girl growing up to know, yes, you can become an astronaut because there's Mae Jemison. But it's important for older white males who sometimes make decisions on those careers of those little black girls.

New York Times (September 13, 1992)

EARVIN (Magic) JOHNSON
(Lansing, Michigan, 1959–   )

Earvin Johnson has played for the National Basketball Association (NBA) since 1979. He was named the NBA's Most Valuable Player three times. He heads the Magic Johnson Foundation, which is dedicated to AIDS research. Johnson rejoined the Los Angeles Lakers in 1996.

432   Don't let anyone tell you what you *can't* do. If you don't succeed let it be because of you. Don't blame it on other people.

My Life (1992)

433   Talent is never enough. With a few exceptions, the best players are the hardest workers.

My Life (1992)

❖ ❖ ❖

JOHN H. JOHNSON
(Arkansas City, Arkansas, 1918–   )

John H. Johnson turned a five hundred dollar loan into a multimillion dollar business empire, becoming one of the richest men in the United States in the process. For decades he has entertained and educated the public with Ebony *and* Jet, *the magazines that are the foundations of his fortune.*

434   I've made mistakes in my life. But God knows I've never been at a loss for a solution, even when it was wrong. A good general always has another plan.

Succeeding against the Odds (1989)

435   There is a wisdom in the body that is older and more reliable than clocks and calendars.

Succeeding against the Odds (1989)

436   There's no balance in the life of money. You either have too much or too little. When you don't have it, you run like the devil to get it. And when you have it, you run like the devil to keep it.

Succeeding against the Odds (1989)

437   You have to change images before you can change acts and instructions.

Succeeding against the Odds (1989)

John H. Johnson. *Used by permission of the Schomburg Center for Research in Black Culture, The New York Public Library. Photograph by Isaac Sutton.*

438   I believe the greater the handicap the greater the triumph.
Succeeding against the Odds (1989)

439   Long shots do come in and . . . hard work, dedication and per-severance will overcome almost any prejudice and open almost any door.
Succeeding against the Odds (1989)

❖ ❖ ❖

VIRGINIA JOHNSON
(Washington, D.C., 1952–   )

Virginia Johnson is among the first members of the Dance Theatre of Harlem. She joined the troupe at the age of nineteen and is now a prima ballerina with the company.

440   I had an interview with the paper in Sacramento. It was a little frustrating trying to explain how much we were all setting out to be excellent ballet dancers, not just black ballet dancers. As if being born black meant being born in a cage and your entire life would be described by that cage. The interviewer, being white and never having experienced that kind of limitation, could not understand.
Personal journal (January 20, 1988), *New York Times* (March 6, 1994)

❖ ❖ ❖

BILL T. JONES
(Wayland, New York, 1952–   )

Dancer and choreographer Bill T. Jones cofounded with Arnie Zane the American Dance Asylum. After Zane's death in 1988, Jones continued the company, gaining great critical acclaim.

441   We're living in a garbage heap. All our values are going down the drain. Nothing matters. But I think I'm finding my faith. Something about making a choice. Do I live or do I die? Well, I'm going to live, and it's going to be a meaningful, affirmative experience.

New York Times (November 4, 1990)

442   Life has made me brave.

People Weekly (July 31, 1992)

❖ ❖ ❖

JAMES EARL JONES
(Tate County, Mississippi, 1931–   )

In his early years, James Earl Jones developed a stutter so serious that he could barely speak. He eventually overcame this impairment and went on to become a fine actor. He has also appeared on television and in films.

443   The odd thing about democracy, in that its key factor is the vote, is that we as a people tend to vote into office what we feel about ourselves—and we have felt corrupt for a long time. . . . I think we've felt unclean ever since wiping out the Native American. It goes back that far.

Atlanta Journal and Constitution (May 14, 1989)

444   I can't say I've been a student of black culture because I don't think it exists. No matter how much we reach back out of our sentiments, it is still only sentimentality to refer to an African-American culture . . . but it is irrelevant because we are now basically European by culture and language, and language is the only thing that defines culture.

Los Angeles Times (September 1, 1990)

445   If you feed on bitterness you can nitpick all the way to your death.

Los Angeles Times (September 1, 1990)

James Earl Jones. *Used by permission of James Earl Jones.*

446   You do not have to travel to a foreign country to be a stranger. That can happen to you at home.

Voices and Silences (1993)

447   There is life beyond racism.

Voices and Silences (1993)

448   You have to summon up enormous grace to live so that the frustrations of racial barriers do not defeat you. You have to command that grace in order to survive in spirit.

Voices and Silences (1993)

449   I have learned that color alone is not sufficient reason for conflict or for connection. Color does not inevitably bond, just as it must not inevitably separate. There is nothing inherently, automatically bonding about skin color. Skin is only tissue, pigment, surface. Skin is not identity.

Voices and Silences (1993)

450   My grandmother ... demonstrated her religious fervor through shouting and other dramatic, exotic behavior at church, and through the hymns she sang all day every day on the farm at home. Depressed the hell out of me.

Voices and Silences (1993)

451   Maybe art cannot always change minds, but art can change hearts.

Voices and Silences (1993)

452   You don't have to be a millionaire to be happy.

Daily News (December 17, 1995)

❖ ❖ ❖

QUINCY JONES
(Chicago, Illinois, 1933–   )

Producer and composer-arranger Quincy Jones was a jazz prodigy. He has left an indelible mark in pop music production, films, and television and is the recipient of over twenty-four Grammy Awards.

453   I graduated from the college of the street. I got a Ph.D. in how to make ends meet.

The Dude (1981)

454   I hate categories. I think they demean people.

Los Angeles Times (November 19, 1989)

455   Make what you'd like to hear first. What turns you on. Because you can't figure out what people are going to like.

Ebony (April 1990)

456   There's a science of the universe that will enable you to project your soul. If you are black, your blackness will be projected through your expression.

Ebony (April 1990)

457   There's no way you're going to live anywhere in America and not feel the pangs of racial prejudice. You still get that *hate* stare from certain kinds of white people, but that's a daily experience from the time you're two years old, and you learn to deal with it.

Playboy (July 1990)

458   My kids . . . are all of mixed blood, but they choose to think of themselves as black, and they're proud of it—not because they don't want to be white but because they relate most deeply to the rich heritage of black culture, with all the heartache and all the joy that go along with it.

Playboy (July 1990)

459   Black music has always been the prologue to social change.

Playboy (July 1990)

460   You don't have to let suffering become your experience in life, and you don't have to pass it along to other people just because it hurts. Learn from it. And grow from it. And teach your pain to *sing*.

Playboy (July 1990)

❖ ❖ ❖

JUNE JORDAN
(New York, New York, 1936–   )

June Jordan is a professor of African-American studies at the University of California at Berkeley. She is the author of several collections of poetry, including Living Room *(1985) and* Naming Our Destiny *(1989).*

461   To believe is to become what you believe.

Commencement address, Dartmouth College (June 14, 1987)

462   I do not believe that we can restore and expand the freedoms that our lives require until we embrace the justice of our rage.

Progressive (October 1989)

463   Poverty does not beautify. Poverty does not teach generosity or allow for sucker attributes of tenderness and restraint. In white America hatred of Blackfolks has imposed horrible poverty upon us.

Progressive (February 1992)

464   There is a terrible trouble across this land because power does not change hands, power does not transfer from the pockets of a calculating elite into the treasury of the common good without a mighty, tightening resistance to such change.

Inside America: "My Perfect Soul Shall Manifest Me Rightly" (1992)

❖ ❖ ❖

MICHAEL JORDAN
(Brooklyn, New York, 1963–   )

Michael Jordan, a member of the Chicago Bulls, is one of the highest-paid and best-known athletes in the history of organized sports.

465   I think sometimes I'm looked upon as not just a black person but as a person. And I think that's totally new ground for us—and for society. I'm happy to be a pioneer. . . . View me as a person. I know my race, and I know you know what my race is—but don't magnify it to let me know what my race is when I already know that.

GQ: Gentleman's Quarterly (March 1989)

466   What distinguishes certain players from others is the mental aspect.

Esquire (November 1990)

467   My bitterest concern is that people view me as being some kind of god, but I'm not. I make mistakes. I have faults. . . . But from the image that's been projected of me, I can't do any wrong. Which is scary. And it's probably one of the biggest fears I have.

Esquire (November 1990)

468   To be successful you have to be selfish, or else you never achieve. And once you get to your highest level, then you have to be unselfish. Stay reachable. Stay in touch. Don't isolate.

Esquire (November 1990)

469   My mother is my root foundation. She planted the seed that I base my life on, and that is the belief that the ability to achieve starts in your mind.

Ebony (May 1993)

470   I find myself looking at my children, just watching them and realizing how fortunate I am. Everything I've done on the basketball court, in business, nothing compares to having them.

Rare Air (1993)

471   That's the game of life, being flexible and open enough to move between different circles of people.

Rare Air (1993)

472   Sometimes in life, things just don't go your way. You just have to use that as energy to move forward. Never give up.

New York Times (April 11, 1994)

❖ ❖ ❖

VERNON E. JORDAN, JR.
(Atlanta, Georgia, 1935–   )

For more than two decades, Vernon Jordan has been an influential spokesperson for the plight of black Americans. He served for ten years as executive director of the National Urban League.

473   America's position in this changing world will depend, in large measure, upon its capacity for renewal and upon our ability to finally come to terms with the problems of race.

"The Bohemian Grove Lakeside Talk," Monte Rio, California

(July 19, 1991)

❖ ❖ ❖

FLORENCE GRIFFITH JOYNER
(Los Angeles, California, 1959–   )

Athlete and Olympic gold medalist Florence Griffith Joyner set records in the 100- and 200-meter track events during the 1988 Olympic Games in Seoul, Korea. In addition to her track laurels, Joyner is the author of several children's books and has acted on television.

474   People want to think that staying in shape costs a lot of money. They couldn't be more wrong. It doesn't cost anything to walk.

And its probably a lot cheaper to go to the corner store and buy vegetables than to take the family out for fast food.

New York Times (July 21, 1993)

❖ ❖ ❖

JACKIE JOYNER-KERSEE
(East St. Louis, Illinois, 1962–)

An Olympic athlete, Jackie Joyner-Kersee is the first American to win a gold medal in the long jump and the first woman to earn more than 7,000 points in the heptathlon.

475   I always say to myself, ''I will never forget what it took to get where I am. I see the struggle. I see the hard times. I would not abuse it by getting big-headed and cocky.'' I always believe God gives it to you and God will take it away if he sees you cannot handle it.

Jet (July 10, 1989)

476   She [her mother] taught me the importance of self-reliance, self-respect, and self-discipline. . . . She instilled in me to never take anything for granted, because life is a precious gift, and the gift of life shouldn't be misused, but treasured.

Ebony (May 1993)

❖ ❖ ❖

YELENA KHANGA
(Moscow, Russia, 1962–)

Yelena Khanga's attempts to track her tangled ancestry have formed the subject matter of this journalist's writings and have made her a minor celebrity in the United States.

477   I thought I would find a monolithic black community in America. The real situation was not so simple and radiant. It was a community like any other, ridden by class, social and other prejudice.

Essence (August 1989)

478   No official delegation exchange, no movies or documentaries, no books or television linkup replace direct communication at the public level.

Essence (August 1989)

❖ ❖ ❖

B. B. KING
(Itta Bena, Mississippi, 1925–   )

Guitarist B. B. King is a member of the Rock and Roll Hall of Fame, a five-time Grammy Award winner, and a living legend.

479   I'm never afraid to play something different.

DISCoveries (December 1989)

480   As long as people come to see me I intend to play until I drop.

DISCoveries (December 1989)

481   If you're just playing 12-bar blues you don't have very much to work with, and so you have to be very good to keep the attention of the people. I'm not meaning to pat myself on the back, but with only three chords to work with for 12 bars and then to be playing 41 years and still have people listening, I think I've been doing pretty good.

Twin Cities Reader (March 28, 1990)

482   A lot of times when you say you're a blues player, people tend not to pay much attention. But if you just go ahead and play and prove what you're doing first then say it, everybody loves it.

New Haven Advocate (February 21, 1991)

483   People talk about the resurgence of the blues, but I don't think it ever went away. It's more a matter of discovery.

Phillip Morris Magazine (Summer 1991)

B. B. King. *Used by permission of the Schomburg Center for Research in Black Culture, The New York Public Library.*

484 I like to feel that I can play many styles of music. And I play it because I enjoy it, and it's alright with me if they call it the blues.

New York Post (October 10, 1991)

485 Folks used to say blues was easy. Anybody could do it. Well, if that were true, everybody should be doing it. But the truth is, everybody can't.

New York Daily News (February 11, 1996)

❖ ❖ ❖

CORETTA SCOTT KING
(Marion, Alabama, 1927–   )

Coretta Scott King emerged as a forceful civil rights leader in the United States after the death of her husband, Martin Luther King, Jr. She founded the Martin Luther King, Jr., Center for Nonviolent Social Change in Atlanta and is in demand as a lecturer both here and abroad.

486 I never thought I was going to save the world, but I felt that I could work and make some contribution to make things better for people who come after me.

Ebony (January 1990)

487 As we move towards equality we must project a bold vision of a future in which people of all races have a fair share of the American Dream. But we have to dare to dream of genuine brotherhood and sisterhood between the races before we can bring it into being.

Ebony (November 1990)

488 All too often those who complain the loudest about racism and politics don't even bother to use the power they have and vote.

Address to the Southern Christian Leadership Conference
annual convention, Richmond, Virginia (August 6, 1990)

Coretta Scott King. *Used by permission of the Schomburg Center for Research in Black Culture, The New York Public Library.*

489   Despite the current threat from the reactionaries who want to roll back the clock of progress, we must stand firm in our commitment to nonviolent action. . . . In so doing we will not only win our freedom, but create a better nation for everyone.

Ebony (November 1995)

❖ ❖ ❖

DONALD KING
(Cleveland, Ohio, 1931–   )

Don King, who rode the coattails of Muhammad Ali two decades ago, went on to become a controversial and prominent promoter in boxing.

490   Once you're educated, no one can steal what's in your mind.

Playboy (May 1988)

491   I try to teach white people about black people because I *know* about white people. I have a Ph.D. in Caucasianism, but they don't know us.

Playboy (May 1988)

492   I learned that I can live without anybody. In its own way that's a kind of freedom that is very difficult to come by.

Playboy (May 1988)

493   I recognize that I want to live and die, if I have to, for America's virtue. I'm not gonna decry what should be—we all know what *should* be. Instead of sitting back and crying about it, I'm gonna try to make it happen by working hard, extolling this country and making it live up to its creed.

Playboy (May 1988)

494   The media always twists anything where black success is concerned. They always want to couple a black's success with a negative association—undesirable conditions, evilness, lewdness, depravity—anything demeaning to black ambition, because it's

Donald King. *Used by permission of the Schomburg Center for Research in Black Culture, The New York Public Library.*

always got to be put in some kind of subordinate capacity in order to justify the superiority of the racist point of view.

Interview (October 1990)

495   I want to deal with my white brother with love, understanding and equality of spirit, not insubordination or supplication. This has been my biggest threat to the system. I'm a member of the system and work within the system, even though I'm unwanted.

Interview (October 1990)

496   Hair that's cut fights back. It rebels. And it always gets the last laugh, continuing to grow even when the rest of you is laid out on the slab.

Sports Illustrated (December 10, 1990)

497   I've had my trauma, my travails, my ups, my downs, but still I've persevered. And I've done it without the gun, the club, or the knife. I've done it with wit and cunning and intellect.

Sports Illustrated (December 10, 1990)

498   The system has to be changed. The Jew was the nigger of Germany. Hitler did what the white America did over here in racism. He did it with propaganda.

Sports Illustrated (December 10, 1990)

❖ ❖ ❖

ANDREW DEWEY KIRK
(Newport, Kentucky, 1898–1992)

Andrew Kirk's Clouds of Joy, a group of singers, toured the United States from coast to coast. Musicians such as Mary Lou Williams, Fats Navarro, and Charlie Parker crossed his path. His travels are chronicled in his autobiography, Twenty Years on Wheels *(1989).*

499   The word "black" as it's used now . . . came into fashion with the militants—Black Power—Black is beautiful—the African heritage. I don't like the word. There are so many different shades. I'm not black.

Twenty Years on Wheels (1989)

500 We've had doors opened to us that were closed when I was growing up. But the thing I remember so strongly is not so much the
prejudice—I had a taste of that—but of people extending themselves to help me. . . . I realized that color has nothing to do with
anyone's personality, either black or white.

Twenty Years on Wheels (1989)

501 We couldn't stay in the white hotels where the white bands
stayed. I'm glad now we couldn't. We'd have missed out on a
whole country full of folks who put us up in their homes, cooked
dinners and breakfasts for us, told us how to get along in Alabama, Mississippi, helped us out in trouble, and became friends
for life.

Twenty Years on Wheels (1989)

❖ ❖ ❖

EARTHA KITT
(North, South Carolina, 1928–   )

*Dancer, singer, actress, and social activist Eartha Kitt has had a suc-
cessful career on Broadway and in television and films. She continues
to perform intermittently as a cabaret entertainer.*

502 God may not be there when you want him but he is always on
time.

Confessions of a Sex Kitten (1989)

503 Truth is a theory that is constantly being disproved. Only lies
seem to go on forever.

Confessions of a Sex Kitten (1989)

504 I do believe in the natural map of life, because aging can be just
as beautiful as being young. And I like the fact that I can look
at myself and see lines and gray hair coming in—because I've
earned every line and every gray hair.

Essence (January 1993)

505   I didn't look for a way through life. I just followed wherever the gods sent me. Whatever situations they offered me. Instead of fighting it, I just lived it.

Essence (January 1993)

506   If you keep your soul clean, you'll wind up a much healthier person, and if you feel good about yourself you usually look it.

Essence (January 1993)

507   It makes me furious when I look at women who are in their 50s and 60s and see how beautiful they are at that age but their beauty isn't as readily accepted. Not only do we have savvy, we have knowledge that we did not have before. And now we know how to use it.

Ebony (October 1993)

508   Every time you walk out on that stage you think you're going to fall off because there's no such thing as being secure in show business. You're constantly living on the edge.

Ebony (October 1993)

509   My soul is clean. I'm still here . . . and I will stay me until I'm dead and gone.

Ebony (October 1993)

❖ ❖ ❖

FELA ANIKULAPO KUTI
(Abeokuta, Nigeria, 1938–   )

Fela is an African superstar, popular composer, singer, and musician. Creator of the vibrant music called Afro-beat, Fela couches his protests in lyrics that wittily and provocatively deal with everything from sex to politics.

510   To have a great nation you need great men. And to be a great man you need a great nation.

Fela, Fela (1982)

511 Creativity, not destruction should be the yardstick of greatness.

Fela, Fela (1982)

512 I don't want to say power corrupts. It's when a man is powerful and unknowledgeable that he misuses power.

Fela, Fela (1982)

513 Man can have complete control of his mind. That's what knowledge is about. To be able to control one's mind.

Fela, Fela (1982)

514 The sanity of the world is going to be generated from Africa through art. Art itself is knowledge of the spiritual world. Art is information from higher forces, by those who are talented. . . . I've been living with my art for 23 years. My music has never been a failure.

People Weekly (December 1, 1986)

❖ ❖ ❖

JACOB LAWRENCE
(Atlantic City, New Jersey, 1917–   )

Jacob Lawrence is considered the dean of African-American art.

515 We are absolutely a people telling stories. It seems like we are born talking and telling people about it.

About . . . Time (February 1995)

516 My life was in the Harlem community. I didn't go outside except to an art gallery or museum.

About . . . Time (February 1995)

517 Those of us who are in the arts are fortunate in that we tend to need to search. That is part of our philosophy. Therefore, you continue to grow and to realize your full capacity as a human being. It is a quality of life.

American Visions (April–May 1995)

Jacob Lawrence. *Used by permission of the Schomburg Center for Research in Black Culture, The New York Public Library.*

❖ ❖ ❖

SPIKE LEE
(Atlanta, Georgia, 1957–   )

Spike Lee is a top black filmmaker. Among his box office successes are School Daze *(1987),* Do the Right Thing *(1989),* Jungle Fever *(1991), and* Malcolm X *(1992).*

518   Any approach I take must be done carefully and realistically. I won't be making any apologies. Truth and righteousness is on our side. Black folks are tired of being killed.

> Personal journal, *Do the Right Thing* (December 27, 1987)

519   Isn't it strange? There has been a recent upsurge in racial attacks in this country. At the same time, Eddie Murphy and Cosby are the biggest names in television and film. What a paradox.

> Personal journal, *Do the Right Thing* (January 23, 1988)

520   Any time a film gets people talking, that's a step in the right direction.

> *Essence* (February 1988)

521   There's nothing wrong with showing stuff that's less than glimmering about ourselves. I don't think every time we do something about black people it has to have godlike qualities.

> *Essence* (February 1988)

522   How can you correct anything if you don't at least acknowledge the problem and try to work on it? Because of that kind of thinking we're still playing this light-skin versus dark-skin stuff. That should have been over a long time ago.

> *Essence* (February 1988)

523   The whole thing comes down to self-hatred. It's exemplified by the weaves, the nose jobs, the blue and green contact lenses and, to some extent, hair straightening. This racism thing is down to

Spike Lee. *Used by permission of Spike Lee.*

a science. They make us hate ourselves and they make money off the self-hatred. Can't get more vicious than that.

Essence (February 1988)

524   I intend to be here for the long haul.

Essence (February 1988)

525   Any black man who is intelligent, opinionated, and who doesn't smile ha-ha, chee-chee continuously, is immediately branded difficult. I'm not difficult, I just know exactly what I want.

Personal journal, *Do the Right Thing* (June 16, 1988)

526   You're as raggedy as a roach. You eat the holes out of donuts.

Sweet Dick Willie, in *Do the Right Thing* (1988)

527   We're not allowed to do what everyone else can. The idea of self-defense is supposed to be what America is based on. But when black people talk about self-defense they're militant. When whites talk about it, they're freedom fighters.

Time (July 17, 1989)

528   Hate is a bitch. When you're hated as a people, you eventually end up hating yourself.

Essence (July 1989)

529   [Bill] Cosby gets my respect if only because he's in control of his creative product. This is the final hurdle for all artists, but it is especially hard-won if you happen to be black. Our greatness, our talent has never been the question. It's been a matter of grappling for control over what we do.

Savvy (October 1989)

530   In order for black people to survive in the 90s we have to stop just consuming and start focusing on owning and controlling our share of America.

Savvy (October 1989)

531   We just want to get this whole different mixture of people, with their heritage, and show how race has everybody mixed up. . . . If you have two black women but one has a short afro and is black, and the other is light-skinned with long hair, eight of 10 black men will choose the light skin.

Village Voice (June 6, 1991)

532 Black people can't be racist. Racism is an institution.

Playboy (July 1991)

533 I've never been one just to blame white people for our ills. We have to take some responsibility. If stuff's going to be corrected it's up to us.

Playboy (July 1991)

534 It has always been my contention that if something is a good piece of work, it transcends all cultural boundaries. That's why I've never had a negative connotation of the word black. I never kept white Americans from loving and stealing our music, dance, or other art forms. Why should it apply to our films?

Playboy (July 1991)

535 White America will never know what it is like to be an Afro-American in this country.

Los Angeles Times (November 15, 1992)

536 As a people we do not need anyone else's stamp of approval.

New York Times (February 22, 1993)

❖ ❖ ❖

MEADOWLARK LEMON
(Wilmington, North Carolina, 1932–   )

Meadowlark Lemon gained fame as a star with the world-famous Harlem Globetrotters.

537 Dad loved me. He wasn't big on saying so, but I knew. . . . I had to be only five or six when he proved he would die for me if necessary. That's a lesson that stays on a kid's mind forever.

Meadowlark (1987)

538 Before I saw the antics of the Globetrotters, football was enough for me. We ran all over the neighborhood, behind cars, up on porches, over fences, behind houses. But when you went around a house to catch a pass, you might find 10 guys waiting to knock your head off. Eventually, you had to get back to where the goal line was, and the farther you ran to avoid contact, the more guys there were waiting for you. I still bear scars from playing those games.

Meadowlark (1987)

539 We played under all sorts of conditions all over the world. In Germany we played at the bottom of a drained swimming pool, with people watching from above. The echo was unbelievable, not to mention the strange bounce on the gently sloping floor.

Meadowlark (1987)

❖ ❖ ❖

SUGAR RAY LEONARD
(Wilmington, North Carolina, 1957–   )

After winning an Olympic gold medal in 1976, Sugar Ray Leonard embarked on a professional career that made him a top boxer.

540 As blacks we fall prey to the myth, the stigma that we can't excel. We tend to use that as a barricade. I always have believed that you can be whatever you want to be if you are willing to sacrifice and dedicate yourself.

USA Today (August 14, 1987)

541 I tell my sons to never take anything for granted; that education is the key to release the shackles of slavery, be it years ago or today.

Ebony (November 1993)

JULIUS LESTER
(St. Louis, Missouri, 1939–   )

Julius Lester's was a forceful voice of the black militant movement during the 1960s. He is author of John Henry *(1994), and* And All Our Wounds Forgiven *(1994). Lester currently teaches at the University of Massachusetts.*

542   In the winter of 1974, while I was on retreat at the Trappist monastery in Spencer, Massachusetts, one of the monks told me, ''When you know the name by which God knows you, you will know who you are.''

I searched for that name with the passion of one seeking the Eternal Beloved. I called myself Father, Writer, Teacher, but God did not answer.

Now I know the name by which God calls me. I am Yaakov Daniel ben Avraham v'Sarah.

I have become who I am, I am who I always was. I am no longer deceived by the black face which stares at me from the mirror.

I am a Jew.

Personal journal (December 1982)

543   In acknowledging our fear, we accept our humanity.
Falling Pieces of the Broken Sky (1990)

544   Education should impress us with how vast creation is and how small we are in the midst of it; and in the acceptance of that is the beginning of wisdom.
Falling Pieces of the Broken Sky (1990)

❖ ❖ ❖

ABBEY LINCOLN
(Chicago, Illinois, 1930–   )

For four decades, the life and career of singer Abbey Lincoln has been one of constant growth. She is a supreme jazz artist and also an actress, composer, and arranger.

545 People don't want to take the time and the courage to venture out and embrace the music for the sake of it. There was a time when art was for the sake of art, and now it's everything for the sake of money, and it has made a great deal of difference in the music.

Tempo (September–October 1991)

546 From both my parents I learned that you can do everything yourself, and you don't have to wait for someone to come and fix it.

New York Newsday (November 17, 1991)

547 I want to lead a life that will be useful for somebody who comes after me, because I got a lot of help from people I didn't know, people who lived and said something. So I take a chance on getting on somebody's nerves. I have to beat it, because they get on mine.

Pulse (November 1991)

548 I am the one who's hard to get along with, who's got a mind of her own. And if you have to run things, run when you see me. Run! Because I'll hurt you. Yes, this is my life. It was given to me by my mother and father and I don't mean to surrender it to anybody. Men, society, anybody. I live for the sake of myself.

Essence (April 1992)

549 You really can't have paradise on top of someone else's misery.

Essence (April 1992)

Abbey Lincoln. *Used by permission of the Schomburg Center for Research in Black Culture, The New York Public Library.*

550   All of the power and everything that anybody has is in me, and I recognize it in everybody else.

Essence (April 1992)

❖ ❖ ❖

LITTLE RICHARD. *See* Richard Penniman.

❖ ❖ ❖

ONNIE LEE LOGAN
(Sweetwater, Alabama, 1910?–)

Onnie Lee Logan was delivered by a midwife, and her mother was also in the profession. Onnie Lee decided to become a midwife after accompanying her mother on her rounds. Onnie Lee developed her gifts and became the most widely respected and sought-after midwife in her region.

551   I'd rather see a baby be born in the world than to eat if I'm hungry. I love it. I'm lookin' at the work of God that man didn't do, and that's something to think about.

Motherwit (1989)

552   White people have done black people wrong. And you know what? They admit it. A lotta 'em that won't admit it knows it. But there's plenty of them that admit it. God did not let it deal with me too much, and I'm glad. 'Cause if you get your mind set on that you cain't go on to nothing else.

Motherwit (1989)

553   It's better to take yo' time. You cain't hurry God.

Motherwit (1989)

❖ ❖ ❖

AUDRE LORDE
(Harlem, New York, 1934–1992)

Audre Lorde incorporated African cultures into her life and art long before the term Afrocentric *existed. Trained as a librarian, she eventually held the Thomas Hunter Chair in English at Hunter College. In 1991 she was chosen New York State poet laureate.*

554   The transformation of silence into language and action is an act of self-revelation, and that always seems fraught with danger.
"Transformation of Silence," paper delivered at the Modern Language Association's Lesbian and Literature Panel, Chicago, Illinois
(December 28, 1977)

555   To survive in the mouth of this dragon we call America, we have had to learn this first and most vital lesson—that we were never meant to survive.
"Transformation of Silence," paper delivered at the Modern Language Association's Lesbian and Literature Panel, Chicago, Illinois
(December 28, 1977)

556   We can learn to work and speak when we are afraid in the same way we have learned to work and speak when we are tired. For we have been socialized to respect fear more than our own needs for language and definition, and while we wait in silence for that final luxury of fearlessness, the weight of that silence will choke us.
"Transformation of Silence," paper delivered at the Modern Language Association's Lesbian and Literature Panel, Chicago, Illinois
(December 28, 1977)

557   For black men as well as black women it is axiomatic that if we do not define ourselves for ourselves, we will be defined by others—for their use and our detriment.
Black Scholar (1978)

558   Oppressors always expect the oppressed to extend to them the understanding so lacking in themselves.

Black Scholar (May–June 1979)

559   For women, the need and desire to nurture each other is not pathological but redemptive, and it is within that knowledge that our real power is rediscovered.

Comments, The Personal and the Political Panel, Second Sex
Conference, New York City (September 29, 1979)

560   Interdependency between women is the way to a freedom which allows the *I* to *be*, not in order to be used, but in order to be creative.

Comments, The Personal and the Political Panel, Second Sex
Conference, New York City (September 29, 1979)

561   Women of today are still being called upon to stretch across the gap of male ignorance, and to educate men as to our existence and our needs. This is an old and primary tool of all oppressors to keep them occupied with the master's concerns.

Comments, The Personal and the Political Panel, Second Sex
Conference, New York City (September 29, 1979)

562   Change means growth, and growth can be painful.

"Age, Race, Class and Sex: Women Redefining Difference," paper
delivered at the Copeland Colloquium, Amherst College (April 1980)

563   It is the response of the oppressed to teach the oppressors their mistakes.

"Age, Race, Class and Sex: Women Redefining Difference," paper
delivered at the Copeland Colloquium, Amherst College (April 1980)

564   My response to racism is anger. I have lived with that anger, ignoring it, feeding upon it, learning to use it before it laid my visions to waste, for most of my life.

Address delivered at the National Women's Studies Association
Conference, Storrs, Connecticut (June 1981)

565   Guilt and defensiveness are bricks in a wall against which we all flounder; they serve none of our futures.

Address delivered at the National Women's Studies Association
Conference, Storrs, Connecticut (June 1981)

566   Anger between peers births change, not destruction, and the discomfort and sense of loss it often causes is not fatal, but a sign of growth.
> Address delivered at the National Women's Studies Association
> Conference, Storrs, Connecticut (June 1981)

567   There is no such thing as a single-issue struggle because we do not live single-issue lives.
> Address delivered at Malcolm X Weekend, Harvard University
> (February 1982)

568   Each of us must find our work and do it. Militancy no longer means guns at high noon, if it ever did. It means actively working for change, sometimes in the absence of any surety that change is coming.
> Address delivered at Malcolm X Weekend, Harvard University
> (February 1982)

569   It is easier to deal with the external manifestations of racism than it is to deal with the results of those distortions internalized within our consciousness of ourselves and one another.
> *Essence* (October 1983)

570   We do not love ourselves. Therefore, we cannot love each other.
> *Essence* (October 1983)

571   What you most of all do not need right now is more rhetoric. What you need are facts you don't ordinarily get to help you fashion weapons for the war in which we are all engaged. A war for survival in the 21st century, the survival of this planet and all this planet's people.
> Commencement address, Oberlin College (May 29, 1989)

572   I am a black feminist lesbian warrior poet doing my work, and a piece of my work is asking how you are doing yours?
> Commencement address, Oberlin College (May 29, 1989)

573   Cheap labor is never cheap for the person who performs it.
> Commencement address, Oberlin College (May 29, 1989)

574   Change did not begin with you, and it will not end with you, but what you do with your life is an absolutely vital piece of that

chain. The testimony of each of our daily lives is a vital missing
remnant in the fabric of the future.

> Commencement address, Oberlin College (May 29, 1989)

575   Our visions are essential to create that which has never been, and
we must each learn to use all of who we are to achieve those
visions. And I am a poet in my bones and sinews.

> *Callaloo* (August 29, 1990)

576   I want my poems—I want all my work—to engage and to em-
power people to speak, to strengthen themselves into who they
most want and need to be, and then to act, to do what needs to
be done.

> *Callaloo* (August 29, 1990)

❖ ❖ ❖

BAABA MAAL
(Podor, Senegal, 1945?–   )

*Baaba Maal, a graduate of the Ecole des Arts in Dakar, Senegal, is the
producer of compelling and beautiful songs of West Africa, at times
mesmeric, stately, and gently stirring. His tenor voice remains unique in
its genre.*

577   In West Africa music is very present in people's lives. Musicians
must take advantage of that to educate their society to point out
the good and the bad. That was the role of the griot in the past,
now it is the role of modern musicians. We must serve humanity.

> *Africa Report* (September–October 1990)

❖ ❖ ❖

JEWELL JACKSON McCABE
(Washington, D.C., 1945–   )

Active in the public sector, Jewell Jackson McCabe served as chairper-son of New York State's $250 million Jobs Training Partnership Council. She has also served on numerous corporate boards and received two honorary doctorates.

578   If I am privileged, then I have a responsibility to pay back.

I Dream a World (1989)

579   The majority of people on welfare are not black, brown or yellow people. They are white people. You factor in racism as a reality and you keep moving.

I Dream a World (1989)

❖ ❖ ❖

LONETTE McKEE
(Detroit, Michigan, 1954–   )

Actress and singer Lonette McKee has been praised by critics for her roles on Broadway and in films.

580   Black actors are tired of the only roles being available to us are the "historically correct" ones of the olden days. Why do we always have to be offered roles where we're housekeepers and slaves. We were, and we have a lot to be proud of, but what about what we're bringing to the table today.

New York Newsday (September 25, 1994)

581   My mother taught me and my two sisters that we had the best of both worlds, the opportunities and advantages of both races. But, in retrospect that was idealistic of her. Now I'd tell kids from a mixed background, "Remember your roots and be proud, but don't be fooled. If you have black blood, in society's terms you are black, and you will be treated as such."

New York Newsday (September 25, 1994)

582 I realized that the only way this society was going to view my calling myself a "mulatto" was as a rejection of my blackness, which was certainly not the case. I'm proud of my black heritage, and I'm proud of my white mother, too.

New York Newsday (September 25, 1994)

❖ ❖ ❖

TERRY McMILLAN
(Port Huron, Michigan, 1951–   )

Terry McMillan, who garnered critical praise for her first novel, Mama *(1987), has since made her mark as a major American writer. Her novel* Waiting to Exhale *(1992) became a best-seller and was made into a movie in 1995.*

583 They [men] keep up this facade, like they've got everything under control. But the minute you get them behind closed doors they fall apart. Once they come to their senses, they say, "Oh, my goodness, she saw my weak side."

Los Angeles Times (June 19, 1992)

584 If you're lucky enough to be given a voice that people want to listen to, I think you ought to use it to say something important.

Ebony (May 1993)

585 I've always had a romantic notion about life, that it was meant to be good; that we have to find our own way; that God puts obstacles in our path to test us, to see what we're made of, to make us pay attention and take notice. If we pass this series of tests we will experience joy, love, a sense of accomplishment, spiritual enlightenment, perhaps even peace.

Essence (May 1995)

586   I don't have to have the answers. I'm just grateful that the questions continue to pop up. Finding resolutions is the best part. And it usually takes awhile.

Essence (May 1995)

587   I question things I can't answer. I lie but try to tell the truth. I can be anybody or anywhere I want to be. I can fake it. I can relive, reminisce, remember, forget, pretend, but mostly embellish. I can resurrect myself and other people's lives. I can get my strength back. I can get back what I think I've lost or find what I'm hoping, praying, looking for. Which is mostly clearing. One clearing after another. I just want to move through the brush and see the sky.

USA Weekend (December 15–17, 1995)

588   It's hard to see the goodness in anything when you're not feeling good inside.

USA Weekend (December 15–17, 1995)

❖ ❖ ❖

TAJ MAHAL
(New York City, 1940–   )

Legendary bluesman Taj Mahal once toured as an itinerant musician working the streets of Spain and playing in coffee houses. He is the composer of several film scores.

589   That's when I started to understand the blues. It takes a bad situation, plays it off everybody and replaces it with lyrical emotional beauty.

Interview (April 1991)

590   As a musician I was interested in playing . . . all I could get my hands on, all I could get my hands around. I kept hearing bits and snatches of songs about the old South, but when I tried to talk to my mother's side of the family, they did not want to talk to me about the South.

Interview (April 1991)

❖ ❖ ❖

MIRIAM MAKEBA
(Johannesburg, South Africa, 1932–   )

In a career spanning more than three decades, Miriam Makeba was a powerful voice in the struggle against apartheid in South Africa. Her music is a soulful mix of jazz, blues, and traditional African music.

591   I look at an ant and I see myself: a native South African, endowed by nature with a strength much greater than my size so I might cope with the weight of a racism that crushes my spirit. I look at a bird and I see myself: a native South African soaring above the injustices of apartheid on wings of pride, the pride of a beautiful people. I look at a stream and I see myself: a native South African, flowing irresistibly over hard obstacles until they become smooth and, one day disappear—flowing from an origin that has been forgotten toward an end that will never be.

Makeba, My Story (1987)

592   My life, my career, every song I sing and every appearance I make, are bound up with the plight of my people.

Makeba, My Story (1987)

593   My hair is very short and natural. Soon I see other black women imitate the style, which is no style at all, but just letting our hair be itself. They call the look the ''Afro.''

Makeba, My Story (1987)

594   It is wisdom, if one has lived one's life properly. It is experience and knowledge. And it is getting to know all the ways the world turns, so that if you cannot turn the world the way you want, you can at least get out of the way so you won't get run over.

Makeba, My Story (1987)

Miriam Makeba. *Used by permission of the Schomburg Center for Research in Black Culture, The New York Public Library.*

595 Africa has her mysteries, and even a wise man cannot understand them. But a wise man respects them.

Makeba, My Story (1987)

596 I don't sing politics: I merely sing the truth.

Los Angeles Times (June 16, 1990)

❖ ❖ ❖

NELSON MANDELA
(Umtata, Transkei, South Africa, 1919–   )

Nelson Mandela has spent his lifetime fighting for the rights of black South Africans, enduring trial and incarceration for his principles. He won the Nobel Peace Prize in 1993. Today he is the president of South Africa.

597 It is a fact of the human condition that each shall, like a meteor, a mere brief passing moment in time, flit across the human stage and pass out of existence.

Address to the joint sessions of the U.S. Congress (January 26, 1990)

598 We must not allow fear to stand in our way. Our march to freedom is irreversible.

Address upon his release from prison (February 11, 1990)

599 The past is a rich resource on which to draw in order to make decisions for the future, but it does not dictate our choices.

Address, King's Park, Durban, South Africa (February 26, 1990)

600 New challenges are upon all people throughout the world. Old problems demand urgent solutions. New problems have to be addressed without delay. The times demand great and not less cooperation among the nations to find solutions to issues that might be national in their specific expression but universal in their essence.

Address, Swedish Parliament, Stockholm, Sweden (March 13, 1990)

Nelson Mandela. *Used by permission of The Bettmann Archive, New York, New York. Photograph by Howard Burditt.*

601 Nothing can stop the evolution of humanity towards the condition of greater and ever expanding freedom. While the voice of an individual can be condemned to silence by death, imprisonment and confinement, the spirit that drives people to seek liberty can never be stilled.

Address, Dail Eireann, Ireland (July 2, 1990)

602 When I walked out of prison, that was my mission, to liberate the oppressed and the oppressor both. Some say that has now been achieved. But I know that that is not the case. The truth is that we are not yet free; we have merely achieved the freedom to be free, the right not to be oppressed. We have not taken the final step of our journey, but the first step on a longer and even more difficult road. For to be free is not merely to cast off one's chains, but to live in a way that respects and enhances the freedom of others. The true test of our devotion to freedom is just beginning.

Long Walk to Freedom (1994)

❖ ❖ ❖

WINNIE MANDELA
(Bizana, Pondoland, Transkei, South Africa, 1934–   )

Winnie Mandela is widely recognized throughout the world as a symbol for the political goals and ideals of the people of South Africa.

603 I *know* he [her former husband, Nelson Mandela] will return to lead the people to his liberation. I *know* he was mandated by the people to lead them to freedom. And *that* task he will come back and undertake.

Ms. (January 1987)

❖ ❖ ❖

WYNTON MARSALIS
(New Orleans, Louisiana, 1961–   )

Trumpeter Wynton Marsalis is a technical genius. As a player of composed music and an improvisor, he is a virtuoso. He is the first instrumentalist to win two simultaneous Grammies in the categories of jazz and classical.

604   The biggest question for our generation is: how do we reconcile ourselves with the traditions of our country and get back to the finest things that make us what we are.

Vogue (August 1989)

605   The whole proposition of the blues is that you *play* the blues to keep the blues at bay. But you know, in your heart, the blues are going to come back anyway.

Vogue (August 1989)

606   Jazz is something Negroes *invented*, and it said the most profound things not only about us and the way we look at things, but about what modern democratic life is really about. It is the nobility of the race put into sound; it is the sensuousness of romance in our dialect; it is the picture of the people in all their glory.

Ebony (November 1990)

607   Artists know that you keep up to date by dealing with the concept of timelessness, which comes from quality. Falsehoods may be in vogue but all they will mean in the future are further examples of how lies were articulated in a particular time.

Ebony (November 1990)

608   Take the time to learn what makes great art and move to support it.

Ebony (November 1990)

609   We now live in an age of aesthetic skullduggery—inside jobs, lying, back-stabbing, theft, larceny. . . . Much of this results from greed and misconceptions.

Ebony (November 1990)

610   The greatest, most emotional works of art have the most complex and rigid form and structure. The question of art is always one of giving order to chaos; that's what makes the artist heroic.

New York Newsday (February 11, 1991)

611   I'm always satisfied with what I do and try to do better next time. It could always be better, you know. It could always be better.

New York Newsday (August 6, 1991)

612   The more you encourage someone else's freedom of expression and the more different that someone else is from you, the more democratic the act.

Washington Post (April 16, 1993)

❖ ❖ ❖

PAULE MARSHALL
(Brooklyn, New York, 1929–   )

Novelist Paule Marshall has worked as a freelance writer and has given lectures on black literature at colleges and universities throughout the United States.

613   I like taking long solitary walks and doing my own things. I'm pretty much someone who lives unto myself—a lover who likes people.

Richmond News Leader (November 15, 1991)

❖ ❖ ❖

THURGOOD MARSHALL
(Baltimore, Maryland, 1908–1993)

During his distinguished career, Thurgood Marshall was in the forefront of the struggle for civil rights and equal opportunities for African Americans. He was the first African-American Supreme Court justice.

614   Racism separates but it never liberates. Hatred generates fear, and fear, once given a foothold, binds, consumes and imprisons.
Liberty Medal acceptance speech (July 4, 1992)

615   The legal system can force open doors, and sometimes even knock down walls, but it cannot build bridges. That job belongs to you and me. The country can't do it. Afro and white, rich and poor, educated and illiterate, our fates are bound together. We can run from each other, but we cannot escape from each other. We will only attain freedom if we learn to appreciate what is different, and muster the courage to discover what is fundamentally the same. . . . Knock down the fences which divide. Tear apart the walls that imprison you. Reach out. Freedom lies just on the other side. We shall have liberty for all.
Liberty Medal acceptance speech (July 4, 1992)

❖ ❖ ❖

EMMA MASHININI
(Johannesburg, South Africa, 1929–   )

Social activism earned Emma Mashinini the deserved fame and reputation, national and international, of being a leading woman in the South African trade movement.

616   Deprivation does a lot to a person. The more you are deprived, the more you are envious of things.

Strikes Have Followed Me All My Life (1991)

❖ ❖ ❖

NOMAVENDA MATHIANE
(Venda, South Africa, 1951–   )

Nomavenda Mathiane was born of Zulu parents. She began her journalist career in 1972 at Drum Publications and has since written for numerous publications, including World, *the* Voice, *and the* Star.

617   That night as I lay in bed, I realized how sometimes a child is born and grows up to shine among people. Eventually when it dies it leaves a trail of blessings to those who have been fortunate enough to come closer to it. And even that makes life worth the pain.

South Africa: Diary of Troubled Times (April 1988)

❖ ❖ ❖

ARTHUR MITCHELL
(New York City, 1934–   )

Arthur Mitchell was one of the first blacks to succeed in classical ballet. In 1969 he founded Dance Theatre of Harlem. The company has earned accolades both here and abroad for its high standards of excellence.

618   By maintaining excellence, I lift my people up. You can be a political activist as an artist, or you can strive to be the best artist you can possibly be, and in that process you are politically active. There's a standard I believe in that I will not relinquish. The way to win the battle is to go in on their turf and do their thing equally well. We are changing perceptions around the world.

Village Voice (August 1, 1995)

❖ ❖ ❖

TONI MORRISON
(Lorain, Ohio, 1931–   )

Nobel Prize winner Toni Morrison is a giant in the literary world. Her prophetic vision of the role of literature in interpreting the African-American experience in the United States is unsurpassed. Included among her works are Beloved *(1987),* Jazz *(1992), and* Playing in the Dark *(1992).*

619   Nothing in the world loves a black man more than another black man. You hear of solitary white men, but niggers? Can't stay away from one another a whole day. So. It looks to me like you the envy of the world.

Sula (1973)

620   My grandfather went to school for one day: to tell the teacher he wouldn't be back. Yet all of his life he read greedily, as did his uneducated friends.

Black World (February 1974)

621   I know instinctively that we do not regard evil the same way as white people do. We have never done that. White people's reaction to something that is alien to them is to destroy it. That's why they have to say black people are worthless and ugly. They need all the psychological ''do'' in order to do something simple like ripping some people off. That's why they behave the way they do.

Black Creation Annual (1974–1975)

622   Children are resilient; and they take what they need from the world and from anyone else they know.

Essence (December 1976)

Toni Morrison. *Used by permission of the Schomburg Center for Research in Black Culture, The New York Public Library.*

623   The memory is long, beyond the parameters of cognition.

Encore (December 12, 1977)

624   I think we really want to be *held*. But we don't know that so we surround ourselves with material things—and they become substitutes for a lack of feeling, of caring.

Encore (December 12, 1977)

625   It is interesting to me that massive bestial treatment did not create a race of beasts. Even the most racist whites, if they could afford it, let blacks take care of their children. You don't let ''beasts'' take care of your children. Black people managed even to civilize slavery.

Encore (December 12, 1977)

626   Black people don't just read. They have to absorb something.

Essence (July 1981)

627   A grown-up—which I think is a good thing to be—is a person who does what she has to do without complaining, without pretending that it's some enormous heroic enterprise. One doesn't have to make a choice between whether to dance or to cook— do both. And if *we* can't do it, then it can't be done.

Essence (July 1981)

628   We have a special insight that can find harmony in what is normally, in this country, perceived as conflict.

Essence (July 1981)

629   Risky, thought Paul D., very risky. For a used-to-be slave woman to love anything that much was dangerous, especially if it was her children she had settled on to love. The best thing, he knew, was to love just a little bit; everything, just a little bit, so when they broke its back, or shoved it in a croaker sack you'd have a little love left over for the next one.

Beloved (1987)

630   The future was sunset; the past, something to leave behind. And if it didn't stay behind, well, you might have to stomp it out.

Slave life—freed life—every day was a test and a trial. Nothing could be counted on in a world where even when you were a solution you were a problem.

Beloved (1987)

631 Black people live all over the world and in all sorts of neighborhoods, but when they think about comfort and joy, they think about one another. That is a vestige of when we thought about staying alive, when we thought about one another.

Essence (October 1987)

632 Now people choose their identities. Now people choose to be black. They used to be *born* black. That's not true anymore. You can be black genetically and choose not to be. You just change your mind, or your eyes, change anything. It's just a mind set.

Essence (October 1987)

633 A novel ought to confront important ideas, call them historical or political, it's the same thing. But it has another requirement, and that is it's art. And that should be a beautiful thing.

Essence (October 1987)

634 A lot of black people believe that Jews in this country by and large have become white. They behave like white people rather than Jewish people.

Time (May 22, 1989)

635 I'm always annoyed about why black people have to bear the brunt of everybody else's contempt. If we are not totally understanding and smiling, suddenly we're demons.

Time (May 22, 1989)

636 The slave trade was like cocaine is now—even though it was against the law, that didn't stop anybody.

Time (May 22, 1989)

637 It's a question of racism, *because* racism is a scholarly pursuit. It's all over the world, I am convinced. But that's not the way people were born to live. I'm talking about racism that is taught, institutionalized.

Time (May 22, 1989)

638   Criticism as a form of knowledge is capable of robbing literature
not only of its own implicit and explicit ideology but of its ideas
as well; it can dismiss the difficult, arduous work writers do to
make an art that becomes and remains part of and significant
within a human landscape.

Playing in the Dark (1992)

639   The scholarship that looks into the mind, imagination, and behavior of slaves is valuable. But equally valuable is a serious
intellectual effort to see what racial ideology does to the mind,
imagination, and behavior of masters.

Playing in the Dark (1992)

640   Deep within the word ''American'' is its association with race.
To identify someone as a South African is to say very little; we
need the adjective ''white'' or ''black'' to make our meaning
clear. In this country it is quite the reverse. American means
White and Africanist people struggle to make the term applicable
to themselves with ethnicity and hyphen after hyphen.

Playing in the Dark (1992)

641   Race has become metaphorical—a way of referring to and dis-
guising forces, events, classes, and expressions, of social decay
and economic division far more threatening to the body politic
than biological ''race'' ever was. Expensively kept, economically
unsound, a spurious and useless political asset in election cam-
paigns, racism is as healthy today as it was during Enlightenment.

Playing in the Dark (1992)

642   You repossess your life when you laugh at the things that try to
destroy you.

Washington Post (October 10, 1993)

643   Oppressive language does more than represent the limits of
knowledge; it limits knowledge. Whether it is obscuring state
language or the faux language of mindless media; whether it is
the proud but clacified [*sic*] language of the academy or the com-
modity driven language of science; whether it is the malign language of law—without ethics, or language designed for the

estrangement of minorities, hiding its racist plunder in its literary check—it must be rejected, altered, exposed.

Nobel Prize address, Stockholm, Sweden (December 7, 1993)

644 It's hard raising children. Your children will try you every moment. You will not win all of the arguments. Be prepared to lose some of them, because if you win all of them your children will never grow up. And sometimes you must be willing to let them fall on their faces.

Essence (May 1995)

645 Capitalism isn't necessarily bad in and of itself. But when it becomes a substitute way of living in the world, it can be so seductive that you end up on a journey of quenching a thirst that can never be satisfied.

Essence (May 1995)

646 If you enjoy your own company, there is no loneliness.

Essence (May 1995)

647 Our friendships with one another are the currency of our lives.

Essence (May 1995)

❖ ❖ ❖

CONSTANCE BAKER MOTLEY
(New Haven, Connecticut, 1921–   )

Constance Baker Motley was the first black woman to be a federal judge. Beginning in 1982, she served for four years as chief judge of the Southern District of New York, and in 1986 she assumed senior judge status.

648 You can't invent events. They just happen. But you have to be prepared to deal with them when they happen.

I Dream a World (1989)

649 The suggestion that women should be equal and have a job that a man might have touches people in a very sensitive way. It is not as readily accepted as the idea of equality of blacks; I think there is much more trouble with that. That's a really deep revolution.

I Dream a World (1989)

❖ ❖ ❖

EDDIE MURPHY
(Brooklyn, New York, 1961–   )

Actor-comedian Eddie Murphy has starred on late-night television, toured and performed before sell-out audiences, recorded several best-selling comedy albums, and played leading roles in blockbuster films.

650 Racism is covert now; they do it behind closed doors. . . . It's natural for white people to feel that way. White people used to own us, and they haven't forgotten that yet. I know I haven't forgotten it. I'm still angry about it.

Playboy (February 1990)

651 My people are the most forgiving people on the Earth.

Playboy (February 1990)

652 Racism is rooted in ignorance. And the more sophisticated a society becomes, the fewer racists we'll have. When you integrate with other cultures, racism gets washed away.

Playboy (February 1990)

653 It's not the public that inspires an artist to create. An artist feels the need to create even if there is no public. If there were no one on the planet I'd still do funny things. I'd just be laughing by myself.

Playboy (February 1990)

654 These are serious times, but an artist has to stay true to himself as an artist. That is the only obligation he has—to his art. And if you are focused on that, it will touch people.

New York Newsday (June 28, 1992)

655   Being an artist and being in show business have nothing to do with each other. Show business is all about making a commotion so that people come and see you so you can make some money. Once you get caught up in the commotion that's not real.

Us (January 1993)

656   All inspiration is from a higher power. The body is a shell. The creative spot is from God. I acknowledge that. You hear voices, everybody does. When you get older, you refer to it as intuition.

Us (January 1993)

❖ ❖ ❖

CECIL MURRAY
(1939?–   )

Cecil Murray is senior minister of the First African Methodist Episcopal church, home of Los Angeles' oldest black congregation. He is an ex-combat pilot and holds a Ph.D. He has led his congregation for over fifteen years.

657   To pretend that you can be poor and racially discriminated against without an explosion sooner or later—that is Disneyland. There is no such existence.

Los Angeles Times (May 3, 1992)

658   Nobody in the 1990s is going to predominate over anybody else on a system of inequity. If the haves do not make room for the have-nots, then nobody will have.

Los Angeles Times (May 3, 1992)

659   Violence solves nothing. Violence always causes more problems than it solves. All violence breeds is pain.

Humanist (November 1992)

660   We don't really practice in politics what we preach in religion; the two seem to be unnaturally at odds when they should be inseparably entwined.

Humanist (November 1992)

661   Whether you are a humanist or a religionist, you must radicalize. One person on fire can make a tremendous difference.

Humanist (November 1992)

❖ ❖ ❖

YOUSSOU N'DOUR
(Dakar, Senegal, 1959–   )

Youssou N'Dour is an international star in the field of popular music that has become known as Afro-pop or World Beat. He is a singer-composer and drummer whose style has been given the name mbalax.

662   In Africa, especially with the griot families, we sing with the stomach to give out something from the inside. . . . We have remained quite traditional until the very last minute before opening out into the world.

Hey You! A Portrait of Youssou N'Dour (1989)

❖ ❖ ❖

JILL NELSON
(New York City, 1952–   )

Jill Nelson has been a journalist for over sixteen years. She is a frequent contributor to Essence, *and her work has appeared in numerous publications, including* USA Weekend, Village Voice, *and* Ms.

663   From a distance, it's easy to start thinking that white folks run things because they're especially intelligent and hardworking. This, of course, is the image of themselves they like to project. Up close, most white folks, like most people, are mediocre. They've just rigged the system to privilege themselves and disadvantage everyone else.

Volunteer Slavery (1993)

664 Initially, doing drugs may be about getting high, but sooner than later it's simply about deadening the pain that comes from living real life on its own terms.

Volunteer Slavery (1993)

❖ ❖ ❖

AARON NEVILLE
(New Orleans, Louisiana, 1941–   )

Aaron Neville is the lead singer of the Neville brothers, the living expression of a multicultural mix. The music of the group reflects African, Caribbean, Creole, jazz, rhythm and blues, soul, gospel, rock, reggae, pop, parade, and funeral bands. These diverse roots have made them a popular band on the pop music scene.

665 When I was coming up, a lot of times I was just singing to myself and wishing I could be heard.

New York Times (May 16, 1993)

666 There's always something to pray for.

New York Times (May 16, 1993)

❖ ❖ ❖

CHARLES NEVILLE
(New Orleans, Louisiana, 1938–   )

See Aaron Neville.

667 I never really cared about recognition. Doing music was the reward. I started with a minstrel show making eight bucks a night three nights a week. But even then there was a link with others in the band, and it cycled around to the audience and came back, and that was the reward. It was a religious experience and later occurred to me that this was my way of communing with God.

GQ: Gentlemen's Quarterly (June 1991)

668 Our parents really interacted with us. They sang songs, we played music together. People came to visit and while visiting they may have brought a musical instrument. . . . Music was a real functional part of everyday life.

GQ: Gentlemen's Quarterly (June 1991)

669 We hope to keep getting more and more people with our music . . . which is a message of love and awareness.

GQ: Gentlemen's Quarterly (June 1991)

❖ ❖ ❖

CYRIL NEVILLE
(New Orleans, Louisiana, 1948–)

See Aaron Neville.

670 The meanest person I ever met in my life was a white nun. Whatever desires you had as a young black person the Catholic schools would pump it out of you. This is why I write the kind of stuff I do. One of my punishments was to kneel before the big white crucifix of Jesus, and sometimes it felt like the blood was dripping off of him and right onto me.

GQ: Gentlemen's Quarterly (June 1991)

❖ ❖ ❖

NICHELLE NICHOLS
(Chicago, Illinois, 1936–)

Singer, educator, activist, futurist, dancer, and actress, Nichelle Nichols is a former star of the original popular television and film series Star Trek.

671   Blatant racism is obvious and stupid, but the evil of most racist actions and comments is in their veiled insidiousness.

Beyond Uhura (1994)

672   For everything we do to make it otherwise, life is never a simple journey. We think we're plotting a course from point A to point B, when in fact practically every step we take is a detour, a digression, a side trip.

Beyond Uhura (1994)

❖ ❖ ❖

JESSYE NORMAN
(Augusta, Georgia, 1945–   )

American soprano Jessye Norman is a great opera and concert singer and performer. She has enjoyed a prolific recording career, with over forty-one albums and several Grammy Awards to her credit.

673   Segregation was bad, but we were protected because we had such loving people looking after us.

Eastern Airlines Review (April–May 1989)

674   Your size on the outside has nothing to do with the size of your voice. What you need is the kind of cavities inside your head, your face, your throat, your chest that will produce a certain sound.

Eastern Airlines Review (April–May 1989)

675   It takes years to get that understanding of how *your* voice works, years before you're able to divorce yourself from that horrible word we call "technique," and are able to release your *soul*.

Eastern Airlines Review (April–May 1989)

676   You don't *hear* yourself when you sing. You feel whether the sound is being produced correctly. If it is, you feel *complete*. . . . It's a great high.

Eastern Airlines Review (April–May 1989)

677   [On fame:] Problems arise in that one has to find a balance between what people need from you and what you need from yourself. . . . In the end, you have to choose from all the choices available to you to do your job properly.

Vogue (March 1993)

678   She [her mother] taught me to care, to dream and to be prepared to work from dawn until dusk (and beyond) for things which are important to me. She is part of all that I do.

Ebony (May 1993)

❖ ❖ ❖

PITIKA NTULI
(Blesbok Masakenga, Azania, 1940?–   )

Sculptor Pitika Ntuli has worked as well as a painter, performance poet, and activist. He has exhibited internationally. His sculpture includes a twelve-foot freestanding stone carving at Swaziland airport and a fifteen-foot stone mural.

679   What is my environment in Britain, in London? It is the media whose lips drip racism, violent cartoons, shit and petrol bombs through letter boxes, the ever-contracting boundaries of progress for black people and black culture punctuated by occasional meadows of love.

Orature–A Self Portrait (1988)

❖ ❖ ❖

ELIZABETH NYABONGO
(Toro, Uganda, 1950–   )

A princess of the kingdom of Toro, Elizabeth Nyabongo has had a varied career, which included the high-fashion world of modeling. She abandoned modeling in favor of public service. She has been an ambassador from Uganda to the United States.

680   This African timelessness, in which past, present and future are interwoven, is born from the notion of spiritual identification with our ancestors. History is not just a vague concept; it is tangible and alive.

Elizabeth of Toro (1989)

681   I was named Bagaaya after strong, fearless women who symbolized the spiritual and temporal well-being of our people. . . . I am freed from fear of anything, including death itself. As I forge ahead, I go on my own—entrusting the next cycle of my life to the hand of destiny.

Elizabeth of Toro (1989)

❖ ❖ ❖

BARACK OBAMA
(Honolulu, Hawaii, 1961–   )

Barack Obama is the son of a white American mother and a black African father from the Luo tribe in Kenya. He is the first African American to serve as president of the Harvard Law Review. *As a lawyer, he is currently active in the civil rights arena.*

682   America is getting more complex. The color line in America being black and white is out the window. That does break down barriers. People can come together around values and not just race.

Crisis (October 1995)

683   I don't think you can legislate the heart.

Crisis (October 1995)

684   In the end we have a sense of mutual responsibility, whether black or white. Our salvation lies not in saying "I'm black" or "I'm white," but in taking responsibility for helping those who are less fortunate.

Crisis (October 1995)

685   I learned to slip back and forth between my black and white worlds, understanding that each possessed its own language and customs and structures of meaning, convinced that with a bit of translation on my part the two worlds would eventually cohere.

Dreams from My Father (1995)

❖ ❖ ❖

ODETTA
(Birmingham, Alabama, 1930–   )

Odetta helped to bring folksongs out of the archives and backwoods and into the mainstream of popular American culture. Work songs, freedom and prison songs, spirituals, and blues are part of a repertoire she sings around the world.

686   Folk music straightened my back and it kinked my hair. What is an Afro or natural today used to be called an Odetta.

I Dream a World (1989)

687   I like being useful. I like what I do to be able to help someone. I called it helping to keep the spirit of those who were on the actual firing lines. I'm not quite sure why educating and entertaining have to be separated.

I Dream a World (1989)

688   Through singing I continue to find myself, and the more I find myself the less I have to deny other people themselves.

I Dream a World (1989)

Odetta. *Used by permission of the Schomburg Center for Research in Black Culture, The New York Public Library.*

HAKEEM OLAJUWON
(Lagos, Nigeria, 1963–   )

In 1993 Hakeem Olajuwon became the first player in National Basketball Association (NBA) history to win the Most Valuable Player, Defensive Player of the Year, and NBA Finals Most Valuable Player in the same season (1993–1994).

689 When you understand the purpose of life and you have a direction and a cause . . . there is no pressure.

USA Weekend (April 28–30, 1995)

690 [On $125 basketball shoes:] People are getting lost about the value. Kids today have to be educated that being the most expensive does not mean [being] the best.

USA Weekend (April 28–30, 1995)

691 I would like to be remembered in my professional career as a true professional, to appreciate that word in the right meaning.

USA Weekend (April 28–30, 1995)

❖ ❖ ❖

SHAQUILLE O'NEAL
(Newark, New Jersey, 1972–   )

Shaquille O'Neal is a top basketball center in the world and an international superstar.

692 I was taught at a young age that if you're not having fun then it's time to go.

New York Times (November 15, 1992)

693 Confidence is knowing who you are.

New York Times (November 15, 1992)

694 When I was little I was kind of a juvenile delinquent, but my father stayed on me. Being a drill sergeant he had to discipline his troops. Then he'd come home and discipline me.

New York Times (November 15, 1992)

695 I won't do anything that'll hurt my body or my mind. I don't believe in it.

New York Times (April 3, 1994)

696 I'm not a legend yet. I just work hard at what I do.

Ebony (March 1995)

697 Parents need to be the role models. My parents were [the people] I looked up to as a kid. And I still do.

Ebony (March 1995)

698 Be a leader, not a follower.

Jet (May 15, 1995)

699 I'm real. I'm myself. Right now it's my time. One day the limelight will belong to someone else.

Jet (May 15, 1995)

700 I wasn't always a terrific athlete. I can remember times when I couldn't run, jump and chew gum at the same time. And I just had to practice, practice, practice. I became a pretty good athlete after hard work.

Interview (May 1995)

701 I always knew I was going to be somebody.

Interview (May 1995)

702 I realize that I am a role model. I realize there are children who look up to me. The best thing for me and other athletes is to stay out of trouble. We just have to do the right thing and say the right thing.

Interview (May 1995)

❖ ❖ ❖

ROSA PARKS
(Tuskegee, Alabama, 1913–   )

By refusing to give up her seat on a bus to a white man on December 1, 1955, Rosa Parks became a symbol of the Montgomery bus boycott. She has come to represent the fullness of time on the continuum of the black struggle.

703   The one thing I appreciated was the fact that when so many others, by the hundreds and thousands joined in, there was a kind of lifting of a burden from me individually. I could feel I was not alone. Some have suffered the physical pain, but some of the pain remains.

Life (Spring 1988)

704   When one's mind is made up, this diminishes fear; knowing what must be done does away with fear.

Quiet Strength (1994)

705   I have learned throughout my life that what really matters is not whether we have problems but how we go through them.

Quiet Strength (1994)

706   No one can effectively fight for justice alone.

Quiet Strength (1994)

707   Four decades later I am still uncomfortable with the credit given to me for starting the bus boycott. Many people do not know the whole truth; I would like them to know I was not the only person involved. I was just one of many who fought for freedom. And many others around me began to *want* to fight for their rights as well.

Quiet Strength (1994)

708   Racism is still alive and will stay with us as long as we allow it.

Quiet Strength (1994)

Rosa Parks. *Used by permission of the Schomburg Center for Research in Black Culture, The New York Public Library.*

❖ ❖ ❖

ORLANDO PATTERSON
(Westmoreland, Jamaica, 1940–   )

Orlando Patterson, a professor of sociology, is author of Freedom, *winner of the 1991 National Book Award for nonfiction.*

709   [On the Clarence Thomas–Anita Hill controversy:] African-Americans must now realize that these hearings were perhaps the single most important cultural development for them since the great struggles of the civil rights years. Clarence Thomas and Anita Hill suffered inhuman and undeserved pain, tragic pain, public ordeal, and they will never be the same again. Nor will we all, for what all Afro-Americans won from their pain, ''perfected by this deed,'' this ritual of inclusion, is the public cultural affirmation of what had already been politically achieved: unambiguous inclusion; unquestioned belonging. The culture of slavery is dead.

New York Times (October 20, 1991)

❖ ❖ ❖

RICHARD PENNIMAN (Little Richard)
(Macon, Georgia, 1932–   )

At the height of his popularity rock 'n' roll superstar Little Richard temporarily quit the scene to become an evangelist. He has been inducted into the Rock and Roll Hall of Fame and received a star on the Hollywood Walk of Fame.

710   Elvis was one of my best friends. We both were young at the same time and we got old at the same time. I wish he was here.

Atlanta Constitution (September 21, 1990)

711   The grass may look greener on the other side of the fence, but it's just as hard to cut.
Atlanta Constitution (September 21, 1990)

712   I really feel from the bottom of my heart that I am the inventor, the architect of rock and roll.
Rolling Stone (April 19, 1990)

713   I enjoyed recording back then [the Fifties] better. You had to play. It wasn't no machines, you just couldn't mash buttons and sound like a band. If you couldn't play, you didn't have no music.
Rolling Stone (April 19, 1990)

714   We were all of us vain back in that time. The young and crazy often need a-spankin' and a-plankin'.
Rolling Stone (April 19, 1990)

715   When I made "Tutti Frutti" they thought I meant "good booty," but I meant "Oh, Rudy." They censored me for everything. My toenails, my eyes, my nose—everything.
Rolling Stone (April 19, 1990)

❖ ❖ ❖

CARRIE SAXON PERRY
(Hartford, Connecticut, 1931–   )

Carrie Saxon Perry was the first African-American woman to become mayor of a major U.S. city (Hartford, Connecticut).

716   Strange thing about oppression, you always believe that the oppressor is going to be a good guy. And it ain't so.
I Dream a World (1989)

717   I believe you have to force change. . . . You have to be committed to long distance and accept the fact that it doesn't happen overnight, and that you're doing it probably for another generation.
I Dream a World (1989)

❖ ❖ ❖

ADRIAN PIPER
(New York City, 1948–   )

Adrian Piper is a musician, artist, performer, writer, philosopher, and teacher. Her top priority has been the establishment of her own social and artistic identity.

718   I am the racists' nightmare, the obscenity of miscegenation. I am a reminder that segregation is impotent; a living embodiment of sexual desire that penetrates racial barriers and reproduces itself. I am the alien interloper, the invisible spy in the perfect disguise who slipped past the barricades in an unguarded moment. I am the reality of successful infiltration that ridicules the ideal of assimilation.

        "Funk Lessons Flying," Washington, D.C. (February 1987)

719   I see racism as a personal problem—a psychological problem, on the level of having problems dealing with one's parents.

        Arts Magazine (March 1991)

720   The most exciting, most innovative work is made by those on the margins.

        Arts Magazine (March 1991)

721   Racism relates to a fear of miscegenation or physical boundary violation experienced in sexuality and sexual intimacy. It has to be dealt with on that level. It has to be about self-analysis now and not about the distanced "other" out there.

        Arts Magazine (March 1991)

722   Change is intrinsically painful.

        Arts Magazine (March 1991)

723   The veneer of good will cracks at the slightest movement. Behind it there is nothing but coiled sentience, waiting to explode and rage at being aroused.

        XVI: Do Not Disturb (1992)

Adrian Piper. *Used by permission of Adrian Piper.*

❖ ❖ ❖

SIDNEY POITIER
(Miami, Florida, 1927–   )

Sidney Poitier was the first black to win an Oscar for the Best Actor Award. He has since become a top star and distinguished himself as a fine director.

724   Most of the scripts I did were written by whites. To require a white person to write only for whites is stupid. To require me to write only for blacks is also stupid. I feel very strongly that writers should write, actors should act, directors should direct.

American Film (September 1991)

725   We suffer pain, we hang tight to hope, we nurture expectations, we are plagued occasionally by fears, we are haunted by defeats and unrealized hopes. . . . The hopelessness of which I speak is not limited. It's in everything. There is no racial or ethnic domination of hopelessness. It's everywhere.

Los Angeles Times (March 8, 1992)

❖ ❖ ❖

ELEO POMARE
(Colombia, South America, 1937–   )

Eleo Pomare is a dancer-choreographer who has toured with his own company, both here and abroad. His works deal with the various levels of black consciousness.

726   Religion is often used to keep people in their places. There is a lot of praying and little doing. You can't pray for change. You have to take steps for change. You can't pray for freedom. You have to take steps for freedom.

Durham (North Carolina) *Sun* (June 22, 1989)

Sidney Poitier. *Used by permission of the Schomburg Center for Research in Black Culture, The New York Public Library.*

727 The same bigotry and unfairness has started to wear an ugly hat again. This generation will rebel and have its share of the blues. They will feel the suffering.

Durham (North Carolina) *Sun* (June 22, 1989)

❖ ❖ ❖

COLIN L. POWELL
(New York City, 1937–)

Colin Powell is best known for his service as chairman of the Joint Chiefs of Staff and national security adviser during President George Bush's administration.

728 Once you have experienced a failure or a disappointment, once you've analyzed it and gotten the lessons out of it—dump it.

Parade (August 13, 1989)

729 As much as I have been disappointed in my lifetime that we didn't move as fast as we might have, or that we still have forms of institutional racism, we have an abiding faith in this country. Hurt? Yes. Disappointed? Yes. Losing faith or confidence in the nation? No.

Parade (August 13, 1989)

730 Forty-five years from now, we will no longer be talking about the first Black this or the first Black that. Hopefully, such distinctions will all be behind us. Wishing won't get us successfully to the year 2035. All Americans must work to get us there. And as always, Blacks must work harder than all others.

Ebony (November 1990)

731 I want you to find strength in your diversity. Let the fact that you are black or yellow or white be a source of pride and inspiration to you. Draw strength from it. Let it be someone else's problem, but never yours. Never hide behind it or use it as an excuse for not doing your best.

Commencement address, Fisk University (May 4, 1992)

Colin L. Powell. *Used by permission of the Schomburg Center for Research in Black Culture, The New York Public Library.*

732   I want you to fight racism. I want you to rail against it. We have to make sure that it bleeds to death in this country once and for all.

Commencement address, Fisk University (May 4, 1992)

733   We need to stop shouting. We need to stop filling our times with filth. We need to start having a sense of outrage at some of the things that are happening in our society that we take for granted.

Address, Trinity University (January 30, 1995)

734   We have to keep our lives on certain fundamental principles, and one of those is that America is a family. We've got to start remembering that no member of our family should be satisfied if any member of our American family is suffering or in need and we can do something about it.

Time (July 10, 1995)

735   Racism has been unfortunately an ingrained part of our society for a couple of hundred years.

Time (July 10, 1995)

736   I'm not sure anyone or anything can live up to the standards the American people are trying to put on their political process, because politics is ultimately debate, fighting, compromise, consensus, and then you get the synthesis you need to move forward. But it isn't always pretty to watch.

Time (July 10, 1995)

737   The one thing none of us can escape, whether we are on the right, left, middle, top or bottom, black, white, brown, green or yellow, is that we are all living in this one country together. . . . We are blessed with each other—stuck with each other. We had better figure out how to get along with each other.

Los Angeles Times (October 9, 1995)

738   It ain't as bad as you think. It will look better in the morning.

My American Journey (1995)

739   Get mad. Then get over it.

My American Journey (1995)

740   Be careful what you choose. You may get it.

My American Journey (1995)

741   You can't make someone else's choices. You shouldn't let someone else make yours.

My American Journey (1995)

742   We are a fractious nation, always searching, always dissatisfied,
yet always hopeful. We have an infinite capacity to rejuvenate
ourselves.

My American Journey (1995)

743   You're going nowhere unless you finish high school. It's the last
time you'll get anything so valuable for free. Stay in school and
stay away from drugs. . . . They destroy the body and sound mind
that God and our parents have given us.

Teleconference, Loyola Marymount University (February 1996)

❖ ❖ ❖

PEARL PRIMUS
(Trinidad, 1919–1994)

*Pearl Primus was considered the grandmother of black dance as an
ethnic study and art. The award-winning performer held a doctorate in
anthropology and educational sociology, and taught dance at her own
school in New York City.*

744   It's a little different for me to dwell upon the past unless its a
springboard to now.

Chronicle of Higher Education (July 1991)

745   [On her motivation as a dancer:] I wanted to speak of dignity,
beauty and strength and heritage of people of African ancestry,
myself having been deeply hurt in a racist society.

Chronicle of Higher Education (July 1991)

❖ ❖ ❖

THE ARTIST FORMERLY KNOWN AS PRINCE
(Minneapolis, Minnesota, 1958–   )

The Artist Formerly Known As Prince is a singer, instrumentalist, song-writer, arranger, producer, and actor. Among his top-selling albums are Dirty Mind *(1980),* Controversy *(1981), and* 1999 *(1982).*

746   When I talk about God I don't mean some dude in a robe and beard coming down to earth. To me, he's in everything if you look at it that way.

Rolling Stone (October 18, 1990)

747   I feel good most of the time and I like to express that by writing for joy. I still do write from anger . . . but I don't like to. It's not a place to live.

Rolling Stone (October 18, 1990)

748   I look for cosmic meaning in everything.

Rolling Stone (October 18, 1990)

❖ ❖ ❖

RICHARD PRYOR
(Peoria, Illinois, 1940–   )

In the 1970s and 1980s Richard Pryor was a top comedian, actor, writer, and stand-up artist whose albums sold in the millions. He dropped from the scene due to alcohol and substance abuse and now appears only intermittently on the cabaret stage.

749   Faster than a bowl of chitlins. Able to leap a slum with a single bound. "Look up in the sky." "It's a crow." "It's a bat." No, it's Super Nigger.

From the album *Who Me? I'm Not Him* (1977)

The Artist Formerly Known As Prince. *Used by permission of the Schomburg Center for Research in Black Culture, The New York Public Library.*

Richard Pryor. *Used by permission of the Schomburg Center for Research in Black Culture, The New York Public Library.*

750 When you have a blackness and you reach out of this blackness into the light, it's just the thought of Him. And you feel that.

Washington Post (December 29, 1992)

751 I just think that we as people sometimes don't be nice to each other. And sometimes we're real good to each other. And I think that's it.

Washington Post (December 29, 1992)

752 I think about dying. I've come to realize we all die alone in one way or another. You can have a room full of people when it's your time to walk into the light, but you can bet your ass not one person will offer to go with you.

Entertainment (April 30, 1993)

753 We had a curfew in my neighborhood. Niggers home by eleven. Negroes by midnight.

Pryor Convictions (1995)

754 In the world in which I grew up, happiness was a moment rather than a state of being. It buzzed around, just out of reach, like Tinkerbell, flirting and teasing and laughing at your ass. It never stayed long enough for you to get to know it good. Just a taste here and there. A kiss, a sniff, a stroke, a snort.

Pryor Convictions (1995)

755 The comedy gods have many tentacles, you know. And they swoop down and touch you at different times. But when they do it's like salvation. Or deliverance. It's as close to flying as a man gets.

Pryor Convictions (1995)

❖ ❖ ❖

QUEEN LATIFAH
(New Jersey, 1970–   )

When rap was at its height, Queen Latifah was a top performer. She has since appeared in such films at Spike Lee's Jungle Fever *(1991), and she has starred in the sitcom* Living Single *on television.*

756   Sometimes I feel pressure because I don't feel I should be responsible for people's kids. I don't feel I should be forced to speak or react a certain way. I don't use music for politics. I do not preach. I don't really take on sexism—but racism, yeah. I experience racism every day.

New York Times (August 25, 1991)

757   Being considered a leader can be a hassle. Some people put you on a pedestal and don't let you be human. It's like they see themselves in you—they see their best self in you and they expect perfection from their best self . . . but I'm no saint. I can slip, just like anybody else.

Los Angeles Times (September 8, 1991)

758   [On rap:] I was attracted to the sound and the content and the freedom of rap. To me, it's like a free art form. It flows—it's smooth. It can be anything you want it to be—harsh, bitter, funny, you name it.

Los Angeles Times (September 8, 1991)

759   People need to stop sleeping. . . . Hip-hop is not a music that you sit down and listen to and that's it. It gives you a lot of answers . . . but it also gives you a lot of questions.

Christian Science Monitor (November 4, 1991)

760   You take rhythm and blues, you take pop, it's so beautiful, the lyrics are beautiful—love, love, love, love, love, you know?— which is beautiful, alright because everybody loves, love. But that's not what the world is all about. Everybody doesn't love everybody.

Christian Science Monitor (November 4, 1991)

❖ ❖ ❖

ROBIN QUIVERS
(Baltimore, Maryland, 1952–   )

Robin Quivers is a popular radio personality in the United States. She appears on the Entertainment Television network's Howard Stern Interview.

761 People who use the word "nigger" mean it whether they are black or white. It was a word coined in slave times to define a new kind of chattel brought to the New World to work the fields, pulling plows and picking cotton. It was not a word that meant a kind of people, it was the word for a new kind of animal. It retains all its meaning today. There is no nice way to use the N word.

Robin Quivers (1995)

762 Despite everything that had happened to me, I still expected that one day I would fall in love even though I had no idea what that was. I watched everyone to see if I could see it. But I don't think that love lived in my neighborhood, or if it did, there was nothing pretty about it. Made me wonder why everyone wanted to fall.

Robin Quivers (1995)

763 In the fantasy of equality finally bestowed by whites, black problems of high crime, illegitimacy and unemployment will just disappear.

Robin Quivers (1995)

❖ ❖ ❖

CHARLES RANGEL
(New York City, 1930–   )

Charles Rangel is an influential and respected congressman (D–N.Y.).
Since his legislative career began many years ago, he has been recog-
nized as dedicated and hard-working.

764   Real freedom won't come just from building more jails and
putting more cops on the streets; it comes from hope.

Rangel Reports (July 1994)

765   When things are not going right, you find someone to blame it
on.

Emerge (September 1994)

❖ ❖ ❖

PHYLICIA RASHAD
(Houston, Texas, 1948–   )

Phylicia Rashad is a dancer and actress. She had a starring role in the
long-running television series The Cosby Show. *She devotes her time to*
lobbying for an improved lifestyle for senior citizens.

766   I'm not one of those people who say "Do what I do 'cause I did
it." They'll all come in their own time. It's not something you
force on people.

Ladies Home Journal (May 1992)

767   I don't feel the effect of years because age, to me, is learning,
and the quest for understanding is more important than how many
wrinkles I have or how high I can kick when I dance.

Ladies Home Journal (May 1992)

❖ ❖ ❖

BERNICE JOHNSON REAGON
(Albany, Georgia, 1942–   )

Bernice Johnson Reagon has been associated with the Smithsonian In-
stitution as a cultural historian for many years. She is the founder and
artistic director of Sweet Honey and the Rock, an a cappella ensemble
that performs traditional music of the African diaspora.

768   There are those of us who were born to straddle. We were born
in one place . . . sent to achieve in the larger culture, and in order
to survive we work out a way to be who we are in both places
we move.

Ms. (March–April 1993)

769   Life's challenges are not supposed to paralyze you, they're supposed to help you discover who you are. They're the prod that
moves you forward.

Ms. (March–April 1993)

770   I have no tolerance for people who skip steps: they're dangerous
to themselves, their work, and everything else. If you want to be
someplace else you have to start walking. Do the steps. I get that
from my mother.

Ms. (March–April 1993)

771   I especially encourage young people to give their stuff away. You
can't even tell what you created until you give it away. This
process has always been with me. Creating and giving it away.

Ms. (March–April 1993)

772   I found that if you avoided everything that was a risk, there would
be many things you'd never learn about yourself.

Ms. (March–April 1993)

Bernice Johnson Reagon. *Used by permission of Bernice Johnson Reagon. Photograph by Sharon Farmer.*

773   You cannot understand Afro-American culture and history if you don't know the sacred history.

Washington Post (December 21, 1993)

774   We've got to face our diversity.

Washington Post (December 21, 1993)

❖ ❖ ❖

ISHMAEL REED
(Chattanooga, Tennessee, 1938–   )

Powerfully imaginative, Ishmael Reed is a controversial writer who chronicles the black experience. Among his works are Poems *(1988),* Japanese by Spring *(1993), and* Airing Dirty Laundry *(1993).*

775   Writing is a weapon for us. It may be a finger exercise for the Establishment, but for us it's a matter of survival. Our literature is about combat and plotting. Brer Rabbit says, "Please don't throw me into that briar patch."

Los Angeles Times (August 19, 1990)

776   The true thought police are corporate sponsors and a minority of men who control public opinion.

Airing Dirty Laundry (1993)

777   I also know that there's no such thing as Black America or White America, two nations, with two separate bloodlines. America is a land of distant cousins.

Distant Cousins (1993)

❖ ❖ ❖

BEAH RICHARDS
(Vicksburg, Mississippi, 1926–   )

Beah Richards is an actress, poet, and playwright.

778 If you go inside where all people are and where the essence of their being is, you are not going to find anything to hang your prejudices on.

I Dream a World (1989)

779 Blood doesn't run in races.

I Dream a World (1989)

780 The time has come for a perception of compassion in this world. What is this orgy of hate we are going into and where is it going to lead us? If hate had been the motivating thing in my life, I would be dead.

I Dream a World (1989)

781 If there is any equality now, it has been our struggle that put it there.

I Dream a World (1989)

❖ ❖ ❖

LLOYD RICHARDS
(Toronto, Ontario, Canada, 1923–)

For many years Lloyd Richards served as dean of the Yale School of Drama and artistic director of the Yale Repertory Theatre. He has made significant contributions to the field of repertory theater and has promoted the works of new playwrights.

782 I don't want anybody to give me something that I have not earned or taken something from me because of that. It may have happened and I didn't know about it, but I would never vouch for that.

Callaloo (Winter 1991)

783 Sometimes not to be alike results in productive work.

Callaloo (Winter 1991)

784 I take my own reactions; I'm an audience. If I begin to try and project for thousands of people, I can do nothing but confuse myself. I respond and I am an audience. And so really I work for me, knowing within me are the seeds of the responses of many different people.

Callaloo (Winter 1991)

785 People want to go to the theatre and go to places where they can see themselves reflected. And if they find that in the theatre that's the place they will go.

Callaloo (Winter 1991)

786 I consider my responsibility to be to fulfill the intent of the playwright in his work, which does not mean necessarily that I literally do that, because sometimes the playwright is not totally conscious of everything that exists in his work.

Callaloo (Winter 1991)

❖ ❖ ❖

HAYWOOD BILL RIVERS
(Morven, North Carolina, 1922–   )

Bill Rivers attended the Art Student's League in New York City and the Louvre in Paris, where he lived for many years. It was there that he helped found Galerie Huit, one of the earliest Parisian galleries specializing in postwar American art.

787 I paint because I love it. But it's painful, too. You don't really know what you're searching for, and when you find something that goes beyond what you're searching for, it's downright rewarding.

Newsday (August 4, 1992)

❖ ❖ ❖

RACHEL ROBINSON
(Los Angeles, California, 1927–   )

Rachel Robinson is the chairperson of the Jackie Robinson Foundation, which she formed in honor of her late husband, the first African-American to integrate major league baseball. A professional in psychiatric nursing, she has held clinical, teaching, and administrative positions.

788   The committed individual can find a way of making a difference.

I Dream a World (1989)

789   Until the masses of people are living decently, none of us have secured our place in America.

I Dream a World (1989)

790   Until Afro-Americans are fully rejoined with Africa, in terms of pride and knowledge of our ancestry, we will never be a whole people.

I Dream a World (1989)

791   We're engaged in a struggle that will be ongoing for generations, I fear. So the willingness to fight back and the psychological stamina and discipline to keep focused on basic goals is essential.

I Dream a World (1989)

❖ ❖ ❖

DIANA ROSS
(Detroit, Michigan, 1944–   )

As lead singer with the Supremes, Diana Ross was part of one of the most popular singing groups in musical history, and she has had more

Rachel Robinson. *Used by permission of the Schomburg Center for Research in Black Culture, The New York Public Library.*

number-one records than any other artist. Ross has also starred in films and was the recipient of a Tony Award for "An Evening with Diana Ross."

792 I believe you have to make your own opportunity. You really have to get going. Get out! Find 'em! Set 'em up! Do 'em!

Essence (October 1989)

793 I just think there's nothing we can't do. I never considered it to be a disadvantage to be a woman. I never wanted to be anything else. We have brains! We're beautiful. We should be able to do anything we set our minds to.

Essence (October 1989)

794 She [her mother] always believed in me.

Essence (October 1989)

795 Instead of always looking at the past I put myself 20 years ahead and try to look at what I need to do now in order to get there then.

Essence (October 1989)

796 I am so excited to be onstage and in the lights, communicating with an audience. The magic lifts me. I feel as if I am levitating, floating out into the room, close to the people. I feel they can know me and that I can know them on a very human level.

Secrets of a Sparrow (1993)

797 We human beings have minds of our own; we are not puppets to be pushed and pulled at somebody else's whim. I have my own thoughts about things, I have my own opinions, and what I finally decide is right for me may not coincide with what you have in mind.

Secrets of a Sparrow (1993)

798 The top—there's nothing at the top except the top. I've never really wanted to feel that I had made it because then, what is there to work toward.

Secrets of a Sparrow (1993)

799 Singing—performing—is a gift. A divine gift.

Secrets of a Sparrow (1993)

Diana Ross. *Used by permission of the Schomburg Center for Research in Black Culture, The New York Public Library.*

❖ ❖ ❖

WILMA RUDOLPH
(Bethlehem, Tennessee, 1940–1994)

At Rome, Italy, in 1960 Wilma Rudolph was the first American woman runner to win three gold medals in the Olympic games.

800 Gold medals are one thing nobody can ever take away, but I would be very disappointed if I were remembered only as a runner, because I feel that my contribution to the youth of America has far exceeded my achievements as an Olympic champion.

Life (Spring 1988)

801 I am not white. I am a black woman, and that is the bottom line. Respect for the intelligence of the black woman is yet to come.

Life (Spring 1988)

❖ ❖ ❖

HELEN FOLASADE ADU SADE
(Ibadan, Nigeria, 1959–   )

Sade is an international pop-soul singer whose trademark is a cool, mellifluous voice. Her albums are among the best sellers of the genre.

802 That's how we learn and progress, by actually performing. But that time away gives you time to be part of life, and then you've got something to write about besides hotel experiences. . . . And then there's time to remember who you are as well.

Pulse (December 1992)

803 I still don't understand why there's such a problem with music marketing. It's a record—put it on the shelves and people will either like it or hate it.

Pulse (December 1992)

804 If people don't care about people that are less fortunate than themselves, then they themselves will eventually suffer, because they will have to bear the repercussions of that crime.

Pulse (December 1992)

❖ ❖ ❖

GLORIA DEAN RANDLE SCOTT
(Houston, Texas, 1938–)

Gloria Dean Randle Scott is the president of Bennett College, Greensboro, North Carolina.

805 Part of the manifestation of racism is that we don't value diversity. . . . Probably never will we really be where we want to be until we can strengthen the value of diversity—not to have a hierarchy, but to accept.

I Dream a World (1989)

806 You can focus on obstacles or you can go on and decide what you do about it. To me, it breaks down to that; you can do and not just be.

I Dream a World (1989)

❖ ❖ ❖

OUSMANE SEMBENE
(Ziguinchor, Senegal, 1923–)

Ousmane Sembene is a major African writer and a well-known film-maker. He has attracted worldwide attention by the quality of his artistic creation.

807 Music, soccer and the cinema are three things that mobilize African people. Everything else, such as religion and politics, is secondary. It is for this reason that I took up filmmaking—to be able to initiate a dialogue with my people and other people as well.

> *Africa Report* (November–December 1990)

808   When people stop thinking, conformity sinks in.

> *Africa Report* (November–December 1990)

809   There cannot be a real revolution if women are not a part of it. And there is nothing more revolutionary than feelings of love.

> *Africa Report* (November–December 1990)

810   All religions suffocate women.

> *Africa Report* (November–December 1990)

BETTY SHABAZZ
(Detroit, Michigan, 1936–   )

The widow of Malcolm X, Betty Shabazz is director of institutional advancement and public relations of Medgar Evers College, New York City.

811   The history of America makes it impossible for African-American children, however "sheltered," to escape the psychic legacy of discrimination and racism, even when they escape the physical aspects of racism.

> *Ebony* (November 1995)

812   While I am conscious of all the earth's peoples, I recognize my responsibility to my own ethnic group.

> *Ebony* (November 1995)

ASSATA SHAKUR
(Queens, New York, 1947–)

Assata Shakur is a product of the turbulent sixties and seventies, when the struggle for black empowerment and civil rights was at its peak. The one-time leader of the Black Liberation Army is in exile in Cuba.

813   You see a picture here—that life is difficult all over the world, but that people are coming together everywhere to try, on their level, on their piece of the earth, to make this a better place.

Essence (February 1988)

814   I feel a kind of hope that is invincible.

Essence (February 1988)

815   A lot of people don't know what that program [COINTELPRO] was all about, that the FBI and other government agencies actually set out to squash the black liberation movement by any means necessary, whether it meant killing people outright . . . imprisoning people—and a lot of those people are still in prison—blacks, Puerto-Ricans, Native Americans. The prisons are used as tools of oppression, and the COINTELPRO program was just one part of it.

Essence (February 1988)

❖ ❖ ❖

NTOZAKE SHANGE
(Trenton, New Jersey, 1948–)

Ntozake Shange is an award-winning playwright.

816   I'm a playwright. But I'm a woman first. I am not a generic playwright. I am a woman playwright. And I would hope that my

Ntozake Shange. *Used by permission of Ntozake Shange.*

choice of words and my choice of characters and situations reflect my experience as a woman on the planet. I don't have anything that I can add to the masculine perception of the world. What I can add has to be from what I've experienced. And my perceptions and my syntax, my colloquialisms, my preoccupations, are founded on race and gender.

New York Times (May 7, 1989)

❖ ❖ ❖

ALFRED CHARLES SHARPTON, JR.
(Brooklyn, New York, 1954–   )

Al Sharpton is a controversial New York City political figure. He is a social activist without peer, dedicated to the civil rights struggle for all Americans.

817 You can't fight for just one group of oppressed people and hate another. It is just inconceivable.

Probe (September–October 1989)

818 Ain't nobody gonna slap me on one cheek and expect me to turn another. If somebody slaps me on one cheek, there are three left—two of his and one of mine. And I choose one of the three. And usually its one of his two.

Probe (September–October 1989)

819 Even in the Broadway theatre, those in orchestra seats pay orchestra fees and those in the balcony pay balcony fees. In our present tax structure, those in the balcony are paying orchestra fees and those in the orchestra are getting free tickets.

New York Times (July 27, 1992)

820 I support the Endangered Species Act, and I think it's criminal what we've done to endangered species. I can identify with them because I'm almost an endangered species myself.

New York Times (May 13, 1992)

❖ ❖ ❖

BOBBY SHORT
(Danville, Illinois, 1924–   )

Bobby Short is a popular cabaret performer. He has entertained at the White House for four presidents and has recorded several albums.

821   Discretion is the most important thing about being a saloon entertainer. Lord knows these eyes have seen a great deal. To sit behind the piano, when the lights are low, the liquor is flowing and people—many of whom are my friends—invite me to join them. You belong to them for the evening. But the rule is: never pass that conversation on.

Quest (September 1989)

❖ ❖ ❖

NINA SIMONE
(Tryon, North Carolina, 1933–   )

During the peak of her career in the 1950s and 1960s, Nina Simone's albums consistently placed her among the top performers of the era.

822   The philosophy in our family was that you didn't outshine anyone; you developed the talent you had, but it was there to be shared with everyone else, not hoarded away.

I Put a Spell on You (1991)

823   The difference between a good professional performance and a great show, one where I would get lost in the music, was impossible to know. It just happened. Whatever it was that happened out there under the lights, it mostly came from God, and I was just a place along the line.

I Put a Spell on You (1991)

824 Anyone who has power only has it at the expense of someone else, and to take that power away from them you have to use force because they'll never give it up from choice.

I Put a Spell on You (1991)

825 Sometimes I think the whole of my life has been a search to find the one place I truly belong.

I Put a Spell on You (1991)

❖ ❖ ❖

O. J. SIMPSON
(San Francisco, California, 1947–   )

O.J. Simpson was inducted into the Pro Football Hall of Fame in 1985. He became the center of a sensational murder trial in 1995 in which he pleaded "not guilty" and was acquitted of all criminal wrongdoing. Correspondence sent to him during the trial is chronicled in I Want to Tell You: My Response to Your Letters, Your Messages, Your Questions.

826 You are handicapping yourself when you accept excuses.

I Want to Tell You (1995)

827 I knew there were white people who would always see me as black, and black people who would see me as not black enough. I decided to do what I wanted to do and not let other people define my life. I would do my best with my abilities and never allow my race to be used as a weapon against me.

I Want to Tell You (1995)

828 When you do your best you have no regrets.

I Want to Tell You (1995)

❖ ❖ ❖

NAOMI SIMS
(Oxford, Mississippi, 1949–   )

Following a modeling career, Naomi Sims went on to create a successful line of wigs, develop a namesake fragrance, write several books, and lecture all over the country.

829   Black women are the most exacting women in the world. We're hard on ourselves. Find quiet time, whether it's for prayer, meditation, cooling out or just thinking cool inner thoughts.

Essence (January 1988)

SINBAD (David Adkins)
(Benton Harbor, Michigan, 1956–   )

Known for his "clean comedy," stand-up comic and actor Sinbad began performing in the early 1980s. He has starred on television and in films.

830   My mother and father taught me everything: integrity, honesty, being responsible. My father said you can't be anything unless you accept responsibility for all your failures. My mother wanted me to have a tough hide but a tender heart. That's why I hate violence.

Parade (September 11, 1994)

831   [On his adopted name, Sinbad:] I was trying to figure out who I was, and I wanted to stay positive. So I picked Sinbad. He didn't have the strength of Hercules, but he could outwit anyone. That would be me.

Parade (September 11, 1994)

832   Nobody owes you anything. But you can go out and take it. With education. Pick up a book and read. Learn your history and everybody else's too. And don't be scared to be yourself.

Parade (September 11, 1994)

❖ ❖ ❖

ANNA DEAVERE SMITH
(Baltimore, Maryland, 1950–   )

Anna Deavere Smith is a powerful and distinctive force in the American theater. With a compassion and hard-hitting honesty, her work explores provocative topics such as racism, identity, and social justice. She is author of Fires in the Mirror *(1993) and* Twilight: Los Angeles 1992 *(1994).*

833   Language is a combat between individuals, a combat with the self. Language betrays us. It doesn't always do what we want it to do. I love that disarray. It's where we're human.

Harper's Bazaar (April 1992)

834   It's ultimately not enough to wear the color of your skin. Kids I taught would talk about being an outcast not because they were light-skinned, but because they didn't talk black.

Los Angeles Times (June 14, 1992)

835   My main concern is theatre; and the theatre does not reflect or mirror society. It has been stingy and selfish and it has to do better.

Los Angeles Times (July 11, 1993)

836   I don't think we have any proof that more words really help us to negotiate and understand. . . . It starts with the heart.

New York Newsday (February 23, 1994)

837   Politicians are not prophets. They're people who try to stay in office.

New York Newsday (February 23, 1994)

838   I think that hope lives in the ability to look at things from multiple perspectives, and I do think that is a human ability.

New York Newsday (February 23, 1994)

839 I feel that some things are underdiscussed in this country, and one of those underdiscussed things is race.

Essence (May 1995)

❖ ❖ ❖

SISTER SOULJAH
(Bronx, New York, 1964–)

Sister Souljah has been a prominent community activist and rapper. Raised by a single mother, she grew up in housing projects, on and off welfare. She was a political activist at Rutgers University and ran a camp in North Carolina for children of homeless families.

840 African people love me because I'm a recording artist; they love me because of my work.

Newsweek (June 29, 1992)

841 There's a point at which money confronts ethics—when it threatens the fabric of white supremacy.

Playboy (October 1992)

842 I think that if people were more aware of their spiritual power, they would have less suffering under this white supremacist system.

Playboy (October 1992)

843 As women, we have a responsibility to correct the things that we do that add to our own oppression.

Playboy (October 1992)

844 I have to teach, pass on information, communicate, fulfill my responsibility to serve and lift my community. Some people accept their responsibility, some people reject it, and some people pretend that they don't even know it exists.

Playboy (October 1992)

845 Developing your mind and your psyche will keep you in control of your own reality.

Right On! (June 1992)

846 No matter how backward and negative the mainstream view and image of black people, I feel compelled to reshape that image and to explore our many positive angles—because I love my people.

No Disrespect (1994)

847 Racism is a disease. It affects whites as well as blacks. It may even be a kind of mental illness. But the effect on black people is greater because we are the victims of it. The effect on whites is severe because it deforms their thinking and gives them a distorted picture of the world.

No Disrespect (1994)

848 Loneliness does not discriminate.

No Disrespect (1994)

❖ ❖ ❖

BRENT STAPLES
(Rural, Virginia, 1951–   )

Brent Staples is a journalist, essayist, and educator.

849 The highway was a gorgeous disappointment. It promised everything and took you nowhere.

Parallel Time: Growing Up in Black and White (1994)

850 Davy's boys sang best on Sundays because they sang with their hearts. They sang to get through the dead boredom of a blue-law Sunday, and back into Monday when the bars and liquor stores

opened again. They drank Thunderbird, two dollars a bottle.
Come Monday, Thunderbird would flow.

Parallel Time: Growing Up in Black and White (1994)

851   The rituals of grief and burial bear the dead away. Cheat those
rituals and you risk keeping the dead with you always in forms
that you mightn't like. Choose carefully the funerals you miss.

Parallel Time: Growing Up in Black and White (1994)

❖ ❖ ❖

ROBERT STAPLES
(Roanoke, Virginia, 1942–   )

*Robert Staples is a leading authority on black family life and has written
or edited over eight books on that subject. Among his works are* World
of Black Singles *(1981) and* The Urban Plantation *(1987).*

852   The issue here is that what is often defined as sexist behavior is
nothing more than men acting in ways in which they have been
socialized to behave.

Black Scholar (March–April 1979)

853   Ultimately, the issue in America is not that of sexism or racism;
it is monopoly capitalism and its impact on human potential.

Black Scholar (March–April 1979)

854   The politics of confrontation can be counterproductive when
practiced in a society of unequals.

Black Scholar (March–April 1979)

855   We are a product of our cumulative experiences and the inter-
pretations we give those experiences. Hence, experience, culture
and perspective are essentially one, unless we consciously separate them, and most people do not.

Black Scholar (March–April 1979)

Robert Staples. *Used by permission of Robert Staples.*

856   Trying to appeal to a woman's mind, instead of concentrating on her body, might be the first step to a more harmonious relationship between the sexes.

Black Scholar (Winter–Spring 1992)

❖ ❖ ❖

JULIE STRANDBERG
(New York City, 1940?–)

Choreographer Julie Strandberg founded the Brown University Dance Program, a division of the Department of Theatre, Speech and Dance. She also established the Rhode Island Dance Repertory Company and the Harlem Dance Foundation, a dance studio and resource center.

857   [On dance:] If you fall you should fall with authority.

Brown Alumni Monthly (February 1991)

858   Americans still don't quite know how to cope with "fun" as a productive way of life.

Brown Alumni Monthly (February 1991)

❖ ❖ ❖

SUN RA
(Birmingham, Alabama, 1912–1993)

In a career spanning sixty years, Sun Ra gained wide notice in the jazz world for encompassing everything from bop to gospel to blues and electronic sounds. In addition to touring and live performances over the years, Sun Ra released close to two hundred albums.

859   I always tell my friends I wouldn't be caught dead on this planet—that's not the real me. I was sent here to change this planet, and I'm gonna do it. I'm in God's impossible projects department.

Washington Post (October 5, 1990)

860 I'm part of the angel race. You got the human race and to err is human, but I don't like to err, so I couldn't say I'm human. . . . I couldn't help human beings as a man . . . but an angel can do a lot of things.

Washington Post (June 6, 1993)

861 I would hate to pass through a planet and not leave it a better place.

Washington Post (June 6, 1993)

862 I tell my Arkestra that all humanity is in some kind of restricted limitation, but they're in the Ra jail, and it's the best in the world.

Washington Post (June 6, 1993)

❖ ❖ ❖

SHARON EGRETTA SUTTON
(Cincinnati, Ohio, 1941–   )

A musician, Sharon Sutton has played in orchestras of Fiddler on the Roof *and the Bolshoi, Moiseyev, and Leningrad ballet companies. She is also an architect and teacher, whose work includes development of K–12 design, an educational program for teachers and art exhibitions.*

863 In my fifty years I have made two strenuous climbs into elite, white male domains—first as a classical musician, then as an architect. The combined reality of my race, gender and class is so tenacious—so insidious—that it has helped me to develop a stubborn resistance to the multiple layers of structural inequality.

Finding Our Voice in the Dominant Key (1991)

❖ ❖ ❖

OLIVER TAMBO
(Bizana, South Africa, 1917–1993)

Oliver Tambo was a South African political activist, lawyer, and national chairman of the African National Congress, which he and Nelson Mandela fashioned into their country's dominant liberation organization.

864   We do not doubt that within our lifetimes the millions still oppressed throughout the world will govern themselves freely.

> *Report of the National Executive Committee to the ANC Annual Conference* (December 17–18, 1955)

865   Every age has its prophet. The immediate conditions of life demand of the peoples that they act in particular ways. And yet each day carries both the burden of its past and seeds of the future.

> Olof Palme Memorial Lecture on Disarmament and Development, Riverside Church, New York City (January 21, 1987)

SUSAN TAYLOR
(New York City, 1946–   )

Susan Taylor is editor-in-chief of Essence *magazine.*

866   Thoughts are energy. And you can make your world or break your world by your thinking.

> *USA Today* (July 24, 1984)

867   Let's stop looking outside ourselves for answers to our problems. *We* are the solution.

> *Essence* (April 1990)

Susan Taylor. *Used by permission of Susan Taylor.*

868   Our greatest problems in life come not so much from the situations we confront as from our doubts about our ability to handle them.

Essence (August 1991)

869   Sustaining balance and inner peace is an ongoing process. We must keep our commitment to make time for communion. And we must keep striving to live from within—to walk, talk and be with God, all day, every day. Then our duties, cares and worries become our lessons and our burdens are made lighter.

Essence (August 1992)

870   Life is a journey in self-discovery. If we're not growing, we're not living fully. Growth requires self-examination. It requires that we slow the pace, step back from our lives and assess where we are and where we want to go, that we create and live the plan that will take us there.

Essence (October 1992)

❖ ❖ ❖

LAWRENCE TERO (Mr. T.)
(Chicago, Illinois, 1952–   )

By sheer guts and dedication, Lawrence Tero became, in his words, the greatest bodyguard in the world, winning the title in 1980 of America's Toughest Bouncer. His career later expanded to include television and films.

871   The white man took the chains off my legs, wrists and body but he placed them around my brain. He shackled my mind by refusing me entrance into schools of higher education and jobs with higher pay and position. Yes, I am still a slave. Even with all of my fame, fortune, money and power, I am still a nigger to the white man. That's why I serve God, because He don't make junk. You see, the white folks made a "nigger" but God made a man!

Mr. T: The Man with the Gold (1984)

872 Everybody's out to beat the system, because the system's out to beat you.

Mr. T: The Man with the Gold (1984)

873 If a teacher is never paid what the teacher is worth, that teacher is not worth what that teacher is paid.

Mr. T: The Man with the Gold (1984)

874 I play or perform better under pressure. Pressure makes champions.

Mr. T: The Man with the Gold (1984)

875 There is only one difference between a rich man and a poor man: the poor man thinks only of his next meal, and the rich man thinks only of the meal that will be his last.

Mr. T: The Man with the Gold (1984)

876 I went a lot of days without food to eat; I went a lot of days and even weeks wearing the same clothing and the only thing that kept me going was my dream.

Mr. T: The Man with the Gold (1984)

877 We know we all want to go to heaven but nobody wants to die.

Mr. T: The Man with the Gold (1984)

❖ ❖ ❖

CLARENCE THOMAS
(Savannah, Georgia, 1948–   )

Clarence Thomas stirred up great controversy when, on the eve of his appointment to the Supreme Court of the United States, he was accused of sexual harassment by a former employee, Anita Hill.

878 I will not provide the rope for my own lynching, or for further humiliation. I am not going to engage in discussions nor will I submit to roving questions of what goes on in the most intimate parts of my private life, or the sanctity of my bedroom. These

are the most intimate parts of my privacy, and they will remain just that: private.

> Statement to the Senate Judiciary Committee (October 11, 1991)

879   And from my standpoint as a black American, it is a high tech lynching for uppity blacks, who in any way deign to think for themselves, to do for themselves, to have different ideas, and it is a message that unless you kow-tow to an old order, this is what will happen to you. You will be lynched, destroyed, caricatured by a committee of the U.S. Senate, rather than hung from a tree.

> Second Statement to the Senate
> Judiciary Committee (October 11, 1991)

❖ ❖ ❖

GAIL THOMPSON
(London, England, 1954–   )

Well known on the British jazz scene, Gail Thompson has led her own group, Gail Force; has appeared on television and radio; and has written for festivals and concerts in England and Europe.

880   Jazz musicians from the States come from a long tradition. You can never do what they do in quite the same way. A British band can play a Basie number note-for-note but it will never sound the same. It will never have that sparkle.

> *Storms of the Heart* (1988)

❖ ❖ ❖

JOHNNIE TILLMON-JACKSON
(Scott, Arkansas, 1926–   )

Johnnie Tillmon-Jackson was founding chairperson and, in 1972, director of the National Welfare Rights Organization. She has traveled to more than eight hundred cities organizing people around social and political issues.

881 There's six white women to every black one on Aid to Families with Dependent Children (AFDC) in this country. But nobody ever talks about that.

I Dream a World (1989)

882 I was 46 years old and in the nation's capital before I was ever called nigger. I politely took off my coat, handed my bag to my attorney, and went and had me a fist city on the man's head. He didn't hit me back or nothin', but he ran.

I Dream a World (1989)

DEBBYE TURNER
(Jonesboro, Arkansas, 1966–)

Debbye Turner won the title of Miss America in 1990.

883 I'm tired of stereotypes. I'm proud of who and what I am—but it's just one part of me. I'd love to be a role model for anyone ... anyone who can take an inspiration from me. I feel it's important to look at people's personalities, not how they look on the outside.

New York Newsday (September 19, 1989)

884 I feel ties to the people who sacrificed to give me the privileges that I have today. I can't be representative of all Black people because I haven't met all Black people. I think it's a gross generality to think that all Black people think alike and feel alike, just as it is to think all white people do. I feel the responsibility as Debbye Turner is to be the best that I can.

Essence (January 1990)

885 Don't limit me to being black because there's so much more to me than that.

Essence (January 1990)

❖ ❖ ❖

TINA TURNER
(Nutbush, Tennessee, 1939–   )

During the mid-1980s Tina Turner made one of the biggest comebacks in recorded annals with Private Dancer, *an album that sold more than twenty-five million copies. She has several films to her credit and is an international superstar.*

886   I patterned myself from classy ladies. I take as much from them as I can, but I take it naturally, because I'm not going to be phony about it.

Vanity Fair (May 1993)

887   Music life was not attractive. It was dirty. It was a chitlin' circuit—eating on your lap. And that's why I don't know, but I knew I didn't want it.

Vanity Fair (May 1993)

888   I do something about my life besides eating and exercising. I contact my soul. I must stay in touch with my soul. That's my connection to the universe.

Vanity Fair (May 1993)

889   I am happy that I'm not like anybody else. Because I really do believe that if I was different I might not be where I am today. You ask me if I ever stood up for anything. Yeah, I stood up for my life.

Vanity Fair (May 1993)

❖ ❖ ❖

CICELY TYSON
(New York City, 1933–   )

Actress Cicely Tyson is well known for her portrayal of Jane in The
Autobiography of Miss Jane Pittman *(1974), for which she won two
Emmy Awards. She has been featured on television and holds a record
seven Image Awards from the National Association for the Advancement
of Colored People.*

890   This constant reminder by society that I am "different" because
of the color of my skin, once I step outside of my door, is not
my problem—it's theirs. I have never made it my problem and
never will. I will die for my right to be human—just human.
I Dream a World (1989)

❖ ❖ ❖

BEN VEREEN
(Miami, Florida, 1946–   )

*Ben Vereen is a versatile entertainer whose talents as a singer-dancer,
comedian, and serious actor have made him a long-time favorite with
theater and filmgoers.*

891   If you don't love yourself, you have nothing to hold on to.
Washington Post (July 29, 1990)

892   We are a hypocritical society. We breed addiction. . . . As we
breed addiction, we must also breed its brother, recovery.
Starlite Times (February 1991)

893   You can't be in the way of divine healing because it's not you
doing the healing; we're nothing but vessels.
Starlite Times (February 1991)

Ben Vereen. *Used by permission of the Schomburg Center for Research in Black Culture, The New York Public Library.*

894   If you wallow in the past, you'll stay there.

New York Newsday (June 27, 1993)

895   When I hit the stage, I'm a walking, talking neon sign. I'm a work-in-progress.

New York Newsday (June 27, 1993)

❖ ❖ ❖

ALICE WALKER
(Eatonton, Georgia, 1944–   )

Alice Walker is an award-winning poet, novelist, essayist, biographer, short story writer, and lecturer.

896   No matter in what anger I have written about the black man, I have never once let go of his hand. Though he has kicked me in the shin many times.

Living by the Word: Selected Writings of Alice Walker (1973–1987)

897   At the root of the denial of easily observable and heavily documented sexist brutality in the black community . . . is our deep, painful refusal to accept the fact that we are not only descendants of slaves, but we are also descendants of slave *owners*. And that just as we have had to struggle to rid ourselves of slavish behavior, we must ruthlessly eradicate any desire to be mistress or "master."

Ms. (November 1986)

898   Who we are becomes more obvious to us, I think, as we grow older and more open to the voices and sufferings from our own souls.

Ms. (November 1986)

899   Imagine the psychic liberation of white people if they understood that probably no one on the planet is genetically "white."

Ms. (November 1986)

900   What the black, the Native American and the poor white share in America is common humanity's love of remembering who we are. It is because the language of our memories is suppressed that we tend to see our struggle as unique. And, of course, our language is suppressed because it reveals our cultures, cultures at variance with what the dominant white, well-to-do culture perceives itself to be.

Living by the Word (1988)

901   I couldn't be a separatist, a racial one, and I can't be a sexual separatist. It just seems to me that as long as we are both here, it's pretty clear that the struggle is to share the planet, rather than to divide it.

I Dream a World (1989)

902   Black people are not used to being loved. And when you show them some real love—as opposed to fake love, where you're just kind of praising this and pontificating about that—they really don't know what to do with it. . . . You get used to being loved by loving, because the response to love is love.

Emerge (September 1992)

903   There are some people who honestly could not conceive of the possibility that you could marry a non-Black person and still love black people.

Ebony (May 1992)

904   All my feelings are clear. I don't hide things. I feel the way I feel, and if you don't like it, tough.

Ebony (May 1992)

905   There's a little voice that's always trying to tell you what is really right. To hear it, you need silence, which is hard to come by. This is the noisiest culture, and that accounts for a lot of mayhem. Some people have no idea there's a voice.

USA Weekend (January 19–21, 1996)

906 Don't sit on your feelings. Listen to them and be brave. The world is such a mess, there's nothing left to lose. You might as well feel what you feel.

USA Weekend (January 19–21, 1996)

❖ ❖ ❖

WYATT TEE WALKER
(Brockton, Massachusetts, 1929–   )

Wyatt Tee Walker was a close associate of Martin Luther King, Jr., during the height of the civil rights struggle. He is minister of the Canaan Baptist Church of Christ, New York City.

907 Sermons do not come out of the air, although sometimes when you are on the receiving end, it seems so.

The Soul of Black Worship (1984)

908 It is absolutely essential to understand that black preaching is aimed primarily at the ear as the route to the heart, as over against being aimed at the eye as the route to the mind.

The Soul of Black Worship (1984)

909 The chief function of prayer in the black religious experience has been to cope with the uncertainties of our continuing North American experience. It has never been easy for us in this land. Relatively speaking, only time and place have changed.

The Soul of Black Worship (1984)

910 Slavery, segregation, second-class citizenship, economic dislocation all are only the specifics of systemic racism which touches every waking moment of our existence and every fiber of our being, one way or another.

The Soul of Black Worship (1984)

911 Praying time in a black worship service is an event all by itself.

The Soul of Black Worship (1984)

912   If you listen to what black people are singing *religiously*, it is a
clue as to what is happening to them sociologically.

The Soul of Black Worship (1984)

❖   ❖   ❖

MARSHA WARFIELD
(Chicago, Illinois, 1955–   )

*Comedienne and actress Marsha Warfield has performed as a stand-up
comic in clubs throughout Canada and the United States. She has also
starred in films and on television.*

913   We're just God's way of playing monopoly. Think of your life
and the people and the struggle, and God's sitting up there eating
popcorn and having a laugh at it all.

People Weekly (February 15, 1988)

❖   ❖   ❖

MAXINE WATERS
(St. Louis, Missouri, 1938–   )

*After serving fourteen years in the California State Assembly, Maxine
Waters was elected to the U.S. House of Representatives from California.
Outspoken in her opinions, she is considered a powerful woman in black
politics.*

914   Older black women have always been so helpful. I think that if
the world is ever going to be changed, that's who's really going
to do it.

I Dream a World (1989)

915   No matter how bad it is, we must be optimistic that people will
believe in the power of people living together and respecting each
other.

Ladies' Home Journal (August 1992)

916 No matter how hard it is we can never give up. We must always believe that this can happen in our lifetime.

Ladies' Home Journal (August 1992)

917 I understand racism. I understand that there are a lot of people in this country who don't care about the problems of the inner city. We have to fight every day that we get up for every little thing we get. And so I keep struggling.

Los Angeles Times (May 16, 1993)

918 I have this thing about life: You fit your lines of action. If I am at a cocktail party, talking nicey-nice, I talk nicey-nice. If I'm in a back room where the fight is on, I know how to say son-of-a-bitch as well as anybody, and will fight as hard as anybody.

Progressive (December 1993)

919 I don't pretend to be happy all the time. I don't pretend to be nice no matter what. I don't take insults no matter what. Some people are trained to do that better than others. When you've basically come from a poor background, you're not really trained that way. I didn't go to finishing school. I really work most from the gut.

Progressive (December 1993)

❖ ❖ ❖

FAYE WATTLETON
(St. Louis, Missouri, 1943–)

A nurse by training, Faye Wattleton went to school in Ohio and New York, where she treated abused children and unmarried mothers. She is a former national president of Planned Parenthood.

920 I do not make any apologies for my manner or my personality. I come from a long line of very strong black Afro-American women who neither bend nor bow. I haven't had very good models in submission.

Los Angeles Times (June 19, 1991)

921   We must trust the people. We must trust each other. We must recognize that private morality should be taught in the home and preached from the pulpit, but it must never be legislated by politicians.

Los Angeles Times (June 19, 1991)

JUNIOR WELLS
(West Memphis, Arkansas, 1934–   )

Junior Wells may be the ultimate blues product of the tough, often violent lifestyle of the ghetto streets of Chicago. Wells has been the top star in the South Side blues turf for the past twenty-five years.

922   My father worked so hard till I used to see him with his hands bleedin'. And didn't have no schoolin', no nothin'. He couldn't read or write his name. All he knew was work, from sunup to sundown.

Living Blues (January–February 1995)

923   I would have marched with him [Martin Luther King] once but he was talkin' that non-violence thing. He asked me was I non-violent. I said "Yeah, I'm non-violent. But I *am* violent if somebody hits me." But I had a whole lot of respect for him. And the people that could walk with him and do that thing.

Living Blues (January–February 1995)

924   I could play just as hard for five or six people as I could for 300. You don't have to have a whole lot of people to do what you got to do.

Living Blues (January–February 1995)

Junior Wells. *Used by permission of the Schomburg Center for Research in Black Culture, The New York Public Library.*

CORNEL WEST
(Tulsa, Oklahoma, 1953–   )

College professor Cornel West is noted for his analytical speeches and writings on issues of morality, race relations, cultural diversity, and progressive politics. Among his works are Keeping Faith *(1993),* Prophetic Fragments *(1988), and* Breaking Bread *(1991).*

925 To be independent is not only to be free but also lonely. Most folks can't stand loneliness.

Sing a Song (1975)

926 To be truly free is to clearly see the depths of life. This demands that you step to the edge of a slippery cliff. Few avoid falling over, and the bottom down below has no cushion.

Sing a Song (1975)

927 Rhythmic singing, swaying, dancing, preaching, talking, and walking—all features of black life—are weapons of struggle and survival. They not only release pressures and desperation, but also constitute bonds of solidarity and sources for individuality.

Prophetic Fragments (1988)

928 To be a Christian is to have a joyful attitude toward the resurrection claim, to stake one's life on it, and to rest one's hope upon its promise—the promise of a new heaven and new earth.

Prophetic Fragments (1988)

929 We must never give up hope. . . . I have hope for the next generation, though I think that they're up against a lot. But I believe in the ingenuity, the intelligence, the beauty, the laughter and the love that black people can give both themselves and others. And that is the raw stuff out of which any major movement for justice is made.

Emerge (October 1990)

930 When you talk about hope, you have to be a long-distance runner. This is again so very difficult in our culture, because the quick fix, the overnight solution, mitigates against being a long-distance runner in the moral sense, the sense of fighting because it's right, because it's moral, because it's just.

WNET Television interview with Bill Moyers (1990)

931 Black people have always been in America's wilderness in search of a promised land.

"Nihilism in Black America," Discussions in Contemporary Culture Series, Studio Museum, Harlem (December 8–10, 1991)

932 Where there is no vision, the people perish; where there is no framework of moral reasoning, the people close ranks in a war of all against all.

"Nihilism in Black America," Discussions in Contemporary Culture Series, Studio Museum, Harlem (December 8–10, 1991)

933 Black experience is particular but it's also part of a universal human experience.

Christian Century (August 11, 1993)

934 White supremacy is so profoundly embedded in American and Western civilization that certainly we can make progress and we can ameliorate things, but it is very difficult to envision a time in which it's completely eliminated.

Black Collegian (September–October 1993)

935 We need leaders—neither saints nor sparkling TV personalities—who can situate themselves within a larger historical narrative of this country and our world, who can grasp the complex dynamics of our peoplehood and imagine a future grounded in the best of our past, yet who are attuned to the frightening obstacles that now perplex us.

Race Matters (1993)

936 Let us hope and pray that the vast intelligence, imagination, humor, and courage of Americans will not fail us. Either we learn

a new language of empathy and compassion, or the fire this time will consume us all.

Race Matters (1993)

❖ ❖ ❖

LYNN WHITFIELD
(Baton Rouge, Louisiana, 1951–   )

Actress Lynn Whitfield is best known for her starring role in The Josephine Baker Story. *The role proved to be the breakthrough movie that propelled her to stardom.*

937   The greatest gift my parents and grandparents gave me was the way they lived their lives.

USA Weekend (March 15–17, 1996)

938   You've got to take a stand for something or you'll go for anything.

USA Weekend (March 15–17, 1996)

❖ ❖ ❖

JOHN EDGAR WIDEMAN
(Washington, D.C., 1941–   )

Novelist and short story writer John Edgar Wideman is a leading chronicler of life in urban black America. He is the author of Fever *(1989),* Philadelphia Fire *(1990), and* Short Stories *(1992).*

939   I am intensely proud of my Afro-American heritage and of my color. But color can also be a cage and color consciousness can become a terminal condition. For more than 350 years Americans identified as black have been using the cage of color to deny and affirm, to elaborate one culture, to refuse another.

Life (Spring 1988)

940 Love Jesus and love yourself and love those who love you, sugar. Those who don't love you don't love theyselves, and shame on them. Nobody but Jesus can save their sorry souls.

Big Mama Presents (1989)

941 My grandmother believed in raising a joyful noise unto the Lord. Tambourines and foot stomping and gut-buck piano rolls and drums and shouts and yes if you could find one a mean guitar rocking like the ark in heavy seas till it gets good to everybody past the point of foot patting and finger popping in your chair, past that till the whole congregation out they seats dancing in the air.

Big Mama Presents (1989)

942 Writing is like breathing, it's like singing, it takes the whole body and mind and experience. It's also anarchistic. I like to write because it allows me to do things my way, to say them my way. So what if everybody else's way is different.

Callaloo (Winter 1990)

943 Art should always be something that to some degree shocks and changes people and contradicts what the king says. . . . Writing, art, is subversion, it turns the world on its head, it makes up things. That's its power, that's its joy.

Callaloo (Winter 1990)

944 Knowing the deep structures of Afro-American culture can tell you more about people than knowing the part of the country that they came from.

Callaloo (Winter 1990)

❖ ❖ ❖

L. DOUGLAS WILDER
(Richmond, Virginia, 1931–   )

On November 7, 1989, Douglas Wilder was elected governor of the state of Virginia, the first black elected in the state since P.B.S. Pinchback in 1873.

945   I've always believed in the art of the possible. I believe there's a difference between braveheartedness and foolishness and I believe in whatever I'm going to do. If I don't see success somewhere through the tunnel of that vision, I don't even bother with it.

Los Angeles Times (February 23, 1990)

946   There will be those who will tell you, you can't make it because of where you live, because of how you look, because of the way you talk. We all have heard that . . . I almost listened.

Address, Armstrong High School, Richmond, Virginia
(April 5, 1990)

947   One of the sweetest gifts that life can bring is knowing who you are.

Address, Armstrong High School, Richmond, Virginia
(April 5, 1990)

948   To be ultimately successful, fiscal responsibility requires social compassion. For in the end, the kind of society we have reflects the kind of people we are.

Richmond News Leader (August 17, 1990)

949   Although we were forced to trudge along for generations in the darkness of injustice and discrimination, the light from within has forever shone, sustaining our spirit, guiding us to where we are today, and it shall light the way to tomorrow.

Ebony (November 1990)

950   Looking to tomorrow, I envision a society in which human beings can see and appreciate the strengths of the many individual threads running throughout the tapestry of American society; threads whose fullest beauty and potential are realized only when interwoven with countless others.

Ebony (November 1990)

951   The demand for excellence is now.

Ebony (November 1990)

952   We must continue what was handed down from our parents and grandparents: that hard work produces good results, that dumb people run absolutely nothing, that poverty can be overcome and that one individual can make a difference.

Ebony (June 1993)

953   Progress isn't about huge new government programs, it's about making people's lives better little by little.

Richmond Times Dispatch (January 9, 1994)

❖ ❖ ❖

RALPH WILEY
(Memphis, Tennessee, 1952–   )

Ralph Wiley is best known for his acerbic writings on racism. He contributes to nationally distributed magazines and has authored Serenity: A Boxing Memoir *(1989) and* Dark Witness *(1996).*

954   Without work, people wither in the soul.

Address, Mount Pisgah C.M.E. Church, Memphis, Tennessee
(January 29, 1989)

955   Being black is a gift from God.

Address, Mount Pisgah C.M.E. Church, Memphis, Tennessee
(January 29, 1989)

956   Why do black people tend to shout? Now there is a question for the ages. Black people tend to shout in churches, movie theatres, and anywhere else they feel the need to shout, because when joy, pain, anger, confusion and frustration, ego and thought mix it up, the way they do inside black people, the uproar is too big to hold.

Why Black People Tend to Shout (1991)

957   Thomas Jefferson had a consort, a sister named Sally Hemmings, a woman of color who bore him at least three children. This may be one reason why these days you don't hear of many white people named Jefferson.

Why Black People Tend to Shout (1991)

958   [On Martin Luther King, Jr., and Malcolm X:] Equality, non-violence and peace, self-sustenance, self-determination and self-defense. Great philosophies got them shot, but they got their message across.

Why Black People Tend to Shout (1991)

959   There are a million black leaders. Maybe more. It's hard to tell because most of us are doing our best to stay out of the newspapers, off television and away from White House state dinners. We have things to do.

Why Black People Tend to Shout (1991)

960   Respect is acted out.

Why Black People Tend to Shout (1991)

961   One thing that amazes me about love is how you find it when you're not fishing for it at all, and can never locate it when you've got all the maps looking.

What Black People Should Do Now (1993)

962   Ethics has nothing to do with journalism.

What Black People Should Do Now (1993)

❖ ❖ ❖

ROGER WILKINS
(Kansas City, Missouri, 1932–)

Author, journalist, lawyer, and social activist, Roger Wilkins has chronicled his life in his autobiography, A Man's Life *(1982).*

963   One of the things about being black is that even now, I have this constant rage.

The Last Word (January 1989)

964   The only thing I absolutely know about the future is that if we fail to strike blows now, we cast forward no sparks to light the way for others who will continue our struggle.

Movements (November 1989)

965   White people don't like to talk about racism because it is ugly. Denial is a central element of racism, and feel-good do-nothing denial was elevated to a high art form over the last eight years.

Movements (December 1989)

966   In this imperfect world, racism remains a major affliction that burdens all Americans—and it hits all Americans right in the self-esteem.

Uncommon Ground (August 1990)

967   We can't save white folks' souls. Only they can do that. The best have to save the rest—but to succeed, they have to work at it every day.

Uncommon Ground (December 1992)

❖ ❖ ❖

CECIL WILLIAMS
(San Angelo, Texas, 1929–   )

Cecil Williams, senior pastor of Glide Memorial United Methodist Church in San Francisco, California has headed his congregation for over twenty-eight years. He has been honored by Time *for his support and unwavering service to African-Americans and people of other ethnic groups. His church has a key position in the activist community.*

968   Liberation is really redemption. You reclaim your life and live it. You release your brothers and sisters to be themselves.

No Hiding Place (1992)

969   There is more to life than just making it. We want liberation and empowerment for all. Liberation means choosing freedom. Empowerment means claiming your power to change.

No Hiding Place (1992)

970   In my hometown I often stood on the boundaries between the races. . . . The contradiction between what I heard and what I experienced in the two worlds rattled my head.

No Hiding Place (1992)

971   Urban America is heavy. We're in pain. . . . The pain is like things that crawl out from under the rock.

People Weekly (September 21, 1992)

972 The appeal to Christian values is being used for political aggrandizement. We don't really practice in politics what we preach in religion.

Humanist (November–December 1992)

973 The issue of racism is being misaddressed or even non-addressed. We wave the flag at it. Politicians moralize about it. The public turns its back on it. Everybody condemns racism, but then with a wink of the eye Caucasians go on to the next item while black men and women continue to live with it every day of their lives.

Humanist (November–December 1992)

974 Power concedes nothing without a demand. I don't think real change comes from the top. The change will come from the bottom—from the demand for it.

Humanist (November–December 1992)

❖   ❖   ❖

CYNDA WILLIAMS
(Muncie, Indiana, 1966–   )

Actress Cynda Williams has been performing as a singer since childhood. She attended Indiana's Ball State University, where she was a theater major. Williams made her screen debut in Spike Lee's Mo' Better Blues *(1990).*

975 Being a light-skinned black woman has not landed me more roles as an actress. Casting agents say they want women who are "pure black." Now just what is that?

I'm not a mulatto, I'm black. My mother is white, but that has no bearing on my experience. I accept my mother for who she is and I accept that part of my bloodline, but it's not the leading force in my life. This has a lot to do with how I was raised, because I was raised as a black woman. My parents have always said, you'll never be half and half. People will never look at you through those eyes. They will always look at you as a black woman, period. You're black, so love it, accept it, and want to be it.

> Remark in *Mo' Better Blues*, companion volume to the
> Universal Pictures film (1990)

❖ ❖ ❖

MARION WILLIAMS
(Miami, Florida, 1928–1994)

Youngest of eleven children, Marion Williams joined the Clara Ward Singers as a teenager. She formed her own group in 1959 and went solo in 1965. Her music was featured in the film Fried Green Tomatoes, *which was dedicated to her.*

976 I don't have nothing against other people and what they do, but I don't want no part of singing secular music. I was offered $100,000 to make one blues record, and turned it down. I sing for the Lord, and that's enough for me.

> Comment, *Washington Post* (July 5, 1994)

❖ ❖ ❖

VANESSA WILLIAMS
(Tarrytown, New York, 1963–   )

Best known for her ten-month stint as Miss America, Vanessa Williams has also distinguished herself as an actress and singer. Her first album, The Right Stuff, *spawned four top hits. Among her television appearances have been* Soul Train, Club MTV, *and* Live at the Improv.

977 When I speak to groups of "troubled" teens I tell them the story of my life. This is what happened to me, this is how I fought through it. What made me strong was believing in myself. If you believe in yourself you can endure anything.

> *Fanfare* (July 10, 1994)

978   Always surround yourself with good people.

Jet (May 15, 1995)

❖   ❖   ❖

AUGUST WILSON
(Pittsburgh, Pennsylvania, 1945–   )

August Wilson is a major playwright. His many honors include two Pulitzer Prizes and five New York Drama Critics Circle Best Play awards. His works include Ma Rainey's Black Bottom *(1984)*, Fences *(1985)*, The Piano Lesson *(1990), and* Seven Guitars *(1996).*

979   I done been through life. Made my marks. Followed some signs on the road. Ignored some others. I done been all through it. I touched and been touched by it. But I ain't never been the same fool twice.

Ma Rainey's Black Bottom (1984)

980   As long as the colored man look to white folks to put the crown on what he say . . . as long as he looks to white folks for approval . . . then he ain't never gonna find out who he is and what he's about. He's just gonna be about what white folks want him to be about.

Ma Rainey's Black Bottom (1984)

981   The blues help you get out of bed in the morning. You get up knowing you ain't alone. There's something else in the world. Something's been added by that song. This be an empty world without the blues. I take that emptiness and try to fill it up with something.

Ma Rainey's Black Bottom (1984)

982   Death ain't nothing. I done seen him. Done wrassled with him. You can't tell me nothing but a fastball on the outside corner.

Fences (1985)

983   I ain't never found no place for me to fit. Seem like all I do is start over. It ain't nothing to find no starting place in the world. You just start from where you find yourself.

Joe Turner's Come and Gone (1988)

984   People kill me talking about niggers is lazy. Niggers is the most hard-working people in the world. Worked 300 years for free. And didn't take no lunch hour.

Two Trains Running (1990)

985   You born free. It's up to you to maintain it. You born with dignity and everything else. . . . Freedom is heavy. You got to put your shoulder to freedom. Put your shoulder to it and hope your back hold up.

Two Trains Running (1990)

986   Love got a price on it. Everybody don't want to pay. They put it on credit. Time it come due they got it on credit somewhere else.

Two Trains Running (1990)

987   It's a testament to the resiliency of the human spirit that despite the conditions we have known, despite all the horrors of slavery, despite the sometimes brutal mistreatment blacks have received in this country, we're still here, still managing through it all to find a way to live life with dignity and a certain amount of nobility.

New York Times (April 15, 1990)

988   Blues is the best literature that we blacks have. It's very articulate.

Los Angeles Times (January 1, 1991)

❖   ❖   ❖

MARVIN L. WINANS
(1958–   )

Marvin L. Winans is a pastor and leader of the top gospel group, the Winans. Since their first album in 1983, they have won over nine Grammy Awards.

989   Christians may love to sing about peace and brotherhood, but the people who run the sacred music business do not always practice what they preach. Nobody likes to acknowledge it, but racism is a big problem in the Christian music industry.

Los Angeles Times (November 24, 1991)

❖ ❖ ❖

OPRAH WINFREY
(Kosciusko, Mississippi, 1954–   )

Oprah Winfrey is a millionaire businesswoman with her own top-rated talk show and movie production company.

990   What I have learned in my life and in my work is that the more I am able to be myself, the more it enables other people to be themselves.

USA Today (February 10, 1987)

991   My race and my gender have never been an issue for me. I have been blessed in knowing who I am, and I am part of a great legacy. . . . I am a seed of the free, and I know it. I intend to bear great fruit.

USA Today (February 10, 1987)

992   The bigger issue for me is making myself the best that I can be.

Essence (June 1989)

993   We will falter unless we know our purpose clearly. My purpose is to do my show every day and to raise the consciousness of people.

Wind Beneath My Wings (June 1989)

994   I am proud of every other black woman before me who has done or said anything worthwhile. Recognizing that I am part of that history is what allows me to soar.

I Dream a World (1989)

995   The only difference between being famous and not is that people know your name.

I Dream a World (1989)

996   Every single bit of pain I have experienced in my life was a result of me worrying about what another person was going to think of me.

Ebony (October 1993)

997   I'm every woman and every woman is me.

Ebony (October 1993)

❖ ❖ ❖

GEORGE C. WOLFE
(Frankfort, Kentucky, 1954–   )

Playwright, theatrical director, and producer, George Wolfe took over the reins of the New York Shakespeare Festival in 1993. He is author of Jelly's Last Jam *(1992) and director of the award-winning* Angels in America *(1993).*

998   Being black is too emotionally taxing; therefore, I will be black only on weekends and holidays.

The Colored Museum (1985)

❖ ❖ ❖

STEVIE WONDER
(Saginaw, Michigan, 1950–   )

Singer, composer-musician, and multifaceted performer, Stevie Wonder's records have sold in the millions. He has appeared on television and in films and is the recipient of countless awards.

999   Even with technology today—the computers, the synthesizers, the sampling and the sequencing—you still have to have some kind of feel for the groove, putting the puzzle together, to make the pieces fit right. No matter what it is, you've got to lock in there. And I learned that that comes from what you have within you.

Rolling Stone (November 5, 1987)

1000   The only way that people will be able to see a picture of unity is through music, through dance and rhythms coming together.

Rolling Stone (November 5, 1987)

1001   The only time we should look back to yesterday is to look at the positive things that were accomplished to encourage us to do better things today and tomorrow.

Rolling Stone (November 5, 1987)

❖ ❖ ❖

ALFRE WOODARD
(Tulsa, Oklahoma, 1953–   )

A stage-trained actress, Alfre Woodard graduated from Boston University and worked in the theater at the Arena Stage in Washington, D.C. She has had starring roles in films and on television.

1002   I believe you can't keep a good thing down. It will rise. It might take five months. It might take 15 years, or you may not live to see it. But what I do and why I do my work, and why I think about it or not, is very very connected.

Ms. (April 1969)

1003   Both my parents worked the land and have a strong sense of community values. I lived a few blocks from people who had no floors. I was brought up with the idea that your own comfort is not the end of the sentence.

Ms. (April 1969)

1004   The press steals your soul. If I could have a career without it, I certainly would.

Washington Post (September 26, 1993)

1005   Everyone must earn her right to be on earth. Mine is acting. What I hope to do with my work is to give people a sense of being nurtured even if it's just a laugh. That's my service.

Essence (May 1994)

❖ ❖ ❖

BRUCE McMARION WRIGHT
(Princeton, New Jersey, 1918–   )

Judge, author, and poet, Bruce Wright has devoted his life to delineating the two systems of justice he believes exist in the United States: one for the white and privileged and another for the people of color and the poor.

1006   It is certain that America's dark citizens are not fleeing this country. Indeed, we have no place to flee. We are Americans no matter what. Our African genes have been diluted; we have become assimilated in everything except our visibility. . . . Whatever our destiny, it will not be discovered in some new Liberia, but only here, in the tenements, projects and urban casbahs of America, as we slowly affect and change the system, making it more benevolent from within.

Black Robes, White Justice (1990)

AUTHOR INDEX

SUBJECT AND
KEY WORD INDEX

Numbers refer to quotations.

as a people (Pryor), 751
as writers (Condé), 165
can endure (Angelou), 36
can function (Hunter-Gault), 393
can learn to work (Lorde), 556
can pay teachers (Collins), 157
cannot afford (B. Cosby), 176
cannot forget past (Graves), 321
can't save white folks souls (Wilkins), 967
couldn't stay (Kirk), 501
do not allow children to fail (Collins), 159
do not doubt (Tambo), 864
do not love ourselves (Lorde), 570
do not regard evil (Morrison), 621
everything W do (Nichols), 672
fall prey (Leonard), 540
have any proof (Smith), 836
have been treating mother earth (M. Jackson), 418
have had doors opened (Kirk), 500
have insight (Morrison), 628
have minds of our own (Ross), 797
have responsibility (Souljah), 843
have to clean house (Evers), 236
have unused political power (J. Jackson), 411
hope to keep getting people (C. Neville), 669
live in an age (Marsalis), 609
must be optimistic (Waters), 915
must continue (Wilder), 952
must define (Etuk), 231
must never give up hope (West), 929
must not allow fear (N. Mandela), 598
must trust people (Wattleton), 921
need behavioral scientists (B. Cosby), 171
need leaders (West), 935
need money to survive (Collins), 160
need to do everything possible (Franklin), 269
need to stop shouting (Powell), 733
never had Black History Month (Hayes), 342
nothing W can't do (Ross), 793
played under conditions (Lemon), 539
sing with stomach (N' Dour), 662
suffer pain (Poitier), 725
tend to close off our souls (Dove), 209
tried to act out things (Gerima), 285
want to be held (Morrison), 624
where W came from (Angelou), 29
WEALTH, don't confuse W (Edelman), 217

About the Compiler and Editor

ANITA KING is a writer-editor-researcher whose interest lies in the arts. She is the author of *Samba and Other Afro-Brazilian Dance Expressions* (1989), *An Introduction to Candomblé* (1987), *Quotations in Black* (Greenwood, 1981), and ''Notes About Music: Schomburg's Sheet Music Collection,'' *The Schomburg Center Journal*, Winter 1984.